The Law Commission Annual Report 2016-17

(Law Com No 378)

The Fifty First Annual Report of the Law Commission

Presented to Parliament pursuant to section 3(3) of the Law Commissions Act 1965

Ordered by the House of Commons to be printed on 14 December 2017

HC 639

Law Commission Annual Report 2016-17

The Law Commission was set up by section 1 of the Law Commissions Act 1965 for the purpose of promoting the reform of the law.

This annual report covers the period 1 April 2016 to 31 March 2017, although we have also included references beyond the reporting period, up to and including 30 October 2017 when the terms of this report were agreed.

Law Commission staff, Chief Executive and Commissioners at our London office

Contents

Chairman's introduction

*To the Right Honourable David Lidington MP,
Lord Chancellor and Secretary of State for Justice*

Commissioners, board members and staff

During the year ending 31 March 2017 the five Commissioners remained unchanged. My colleagues are Professor Nick Hopkins (property, family and trust law), Stephen Lewis (commercial and common law), Professor David Ormerod QC (criminal law) and Nicholas Paines QC (public law and Welsh law). Nicholas Paines has also been the lead Commissioner for projects specific to Wales, and last year was designated as Commissioner for Public Law and Welsh Law.

Following the recommendations of a Triennial Review into the workings and governance of the Law Commission, Sir David Bell KCB was, as noted in the last annual report, appointed in 2015 as our first non-executive board member (NEBM). He has now been joined as from November 2016 by Bronwen Maddox. Bronwen is a former Chief Foreign Correspondent of The Times and editor of Prospect Magazine, who is now Director of the respected and influential think tank the Institute for Government. Our two NEBMs assist in the governance of the Commission, offering constructive challenge based on their wide experience. They are not responsible for the choice of our projects, nor for the contents of our consultation papers and reports. We are fortunate to have wise advice from two such distinguished colleagues.

On 31 May 2016 Phil Golding joined us as Chief Executive. His career to date includes tours of duty in the Private Offices of the Lord Chancellor and the Senior Presiding Judge, a year at the Law Commission as Head of Corporate Services, and work for HM Courts and Tribunals Service as head of the administration team running criminal courts in South West England. He also sits as a lay magistrate in Kent. He has brought to the post his energy, experience and commitment to public service, and has already had a major and positive impact on the work of the Commission.

After more than 10 years' outstanding service as team manager for commercial and common law, Tamara (Tammy) Goriely retired from that position but, following a three-month sabbatical, has returned to work part time at the Commission as Head of Policy in the commercial and common law team. Laura Burgoyne has taken her place. David Connolly continues as team manager for public law and Welsh law; Jessica Uguccioni for criminal law; and Matthew Jolley for property, family and trust law. Matthew has in addition been appointed Head of Legal Services, with a particular role in assembling the Commission's 13th Programme of Law Reform.

Jessica de Mounteney continues as our senior in-house Parliamentary Counsel and Vindelyn Smith-Hillman as the Commission's economist. Julia Jarzabkowski remains responsible for statute law repeals, although during the year under review she was in fact assisting with the Intellectual Property (Unjustified Threats) Bill noted below. I have to note with regret that the draft Statute Law Repeals Bill produced by the Law Commission in 2015 has not been introduced into Parliament.

The Commission is extremely fortunate to have at its disposal such a talented cadre of senior staff.

Our corporate services team (CST) – that is to say our support staff who are not lawyers – has undergone streamlining and transformation. Eight members of the team, with a total length of service of 142 years, have left us either on retirement or on moving to posts elsewhere. Our thanks go to all of them for their loyal service to the Commission. The new CST is led by Gulzar Gill as team manager. Patrick Coyne joined us as Head of Communications in January 2017. The members of the new CST are already making a very positive contribution to our work.

Four statutory provisions enacted during or just after the year under review gave effect to recommendations in reports of the Commission.

Part 5 of the Enterprise Act 2016 gave effect to one outstanding recommendation from our 2014 report on the law of insurance contracts which had not been included in the Insurance Act 2015. It gives a remedy to a policy holder who has sustained further loss from an insurer's unreasonable delay in payment of a claim. This reform was enacted with cross party support in both Houses and came into force on 4 May 2017 as section 13A of the 2015 Act.

Part 6 of the Policing and Crime Act 2017 gave effect to our report on pressing problems in firearms law published in December 2015, including closing a loophole which allowed defendants to rely on an exemption for possession of antique firearms even if the weapon was fully effective.

The Intellectual Property (Unjustified Threats) Act 2017, which had been introduced in the House of Lords under the special procedure for Law Commission Bills, completed its passage through the House of Commons on 21 March 2017 and received the Royal Assent on 27 April 2017, the last sitting day before the dissolution of Parliament.

Part 2 of the Digital Economy Act 2017, also enacted at the end of the last Parliament, implemented (with some modifications) our recommendations for a modernised, simplified and more efficient Electronic Communications Code.

It is obvious that during the period leading up to British withdrawal from the European Union pressure on Parliamentary time will be even greater than usual. This makes the special procedure for Law Commission Bills particularly valuable, ensuring as it does that the main work of scrutiny is carried out by a Special Public Bill Committee of the House of Lords and only a bare minimum of "floor time" is needed, especially in the House of Commons.

Constitution Committee

On 21 December 2016 Professor David Ormerod and I gave oral evidence to the House of Lords Select Committee on the Constitution as part of its inquiry into the legislative process.[1] The Law Commission also submitted written evidence. The committee took a particular interest in codification and consolidation. Our evidence dealt with the work being done to prepare, in the form of a consolidation Bill, a Sentencing Procedure Code which would streamline and codify the mass of legislation on the subject. We also argued that it would be highly desirable for the notoriously long and complex Immigration Rules to be streamlined and made more coherent, and for the primary legislation on immigration to be consolidated in due course.

In its report The Legislative Process: Preparing Legislation for Parliament,[2] published on 25 October 2017, the select committee recommended that "the Government should, as a priority, provide the Law Commission with the necessary resources to start consolidating those areas of the law where consistent application of the law is now under threat from the sheer complexity of the statute book", mentioning immigration and sentencing law in particular.

13th Programme of Law Reform

The public consultation on what projects should be included in our 13th Programme began with a launch event at the Supreme Court on 11 July 2016. The keynote speakers were the then Deputy President of the Supreme Court, and former Law Commissioner, Baroness Hale of Richmond and the Attorney General, Rt Hon Jeremy Wright QC MP. The level of response to the consultation was higher than ever before. There were over 1,300 suggestions

1 http://data.parliament.uk/writtenevidence/committeeevidence.svc/evidencedocument/constitution-committee/legislative-process/oral/44752.pdf.

2 https://publications.parliament.uk/pa/ld201719/ldselect/ldconst/27/27.pdf.

covering 220 different subjects by the time the consultation period closed in October 2016. We are grateful to all those who took the time to respond to the consultation.

The selection by the Commissioners of a project for inclusion in a programme requires first that our staff seek an indication from the department with policy responsibility – not necessarily the Ministry of Justice (MoJ) – of a serious intention to take forward reform in the relevant area of the law, as required by the 2010 Protocol between the Lord Chancellor and the Law Commission. Such an indication does not, of course, amount to an undertaking by the Government to bring forward legislation to enact whatever the Law Commission recommends. But it does require the relevant department to agree that there is a problem which needs looking at.

Our original intention had been for the Commissioners, having obtained the necessary indications from departments, to select projects for inclusion in the 13th Programme and submit the draft for your approval in June or July 2017. Discussions with departments about particular projects were well advanced when on 18 April 2017 the Prime Minister announced that (subject to the approval of the House of Commons, which was duly given) a general election would be held on 8 June 2017. This led to the imposition of a period of "purdah" across the public service, during which ministers were not permitted to make decisions except on matters of great urgency. Discussions about the next programme had to be put on hold until after the election, and after that until new ministers had been briefed. The delay to our future planning has been unwelcome but unavoidable. We submitted our proposed 13th Programme to the Lord Chancellor on 10 November 2017. In the meantime our work on current projects has not been affected.

Wales

One of the most important Law Commission reports of recent years, Form and Accessibility of the Law Applicable in Wales, was published in June 2016. It was a project initiated by the Commission when my predecessor Sir David (now Lord) Lloyd Jones was the chair and should be highly influential both inside and outside Wales. The Welsh Government gave its initial response in December 2016 and on 19 July 2017 the then Counsel General, Mick Antoniw AM, wrote to me[3] enclosing the final response.[4] For more information on this project, see page 30.

Our 12th Programme included a project on planning law in Wales for which we have been fortunate to secure the services of Dr Charles Mynors as consultant lawyer. The aim is to create a concise Planning Code accessible and intelligible to non-lawyers as well as lawyers to replace the vast bulk of planning law to be found in Westminster statutes, Cardiff statutes, circulars, guidance notes and a mass of case law. We expect to issue a consultation paper in November 2017.

Nicholas Paines and I gave evidence before the Constitutional and Legislative Affairs Committee (CLAC) of the Welsh Assembly on 5 December 2016. We have also held meetings with the First Minister of Wales, the Rt Hon Carwyn Jones AM; the Llywydd (Presiding Officer) of the National Assembly, Elin Jones AM; the Counsel General; and the Welsh Language Commissioner, Meri Huws. We also took part in the annual Legal Wales conference, which is now a firm fixture in the Law Commission calendar. Our relationship with Wales is important to the Commission and we are grateful to all those, particularly members of our Welsh Advisory Committee, who have given their time to support our work.

3 https://s3-eu-west-2.amazonaws.com/lawcom-prod-storage-11jsxou24uy7q/uploads/2016/06/2017-07-19-Law-Commission-Final-Response.pdf.

4 https://s3-eu-west-2.amazonaws.com/lawcom-prod-storage-11jsxou24uy7q/uploads/2016/06/2017-07-19-Law-Commission-Final-Response-Annex.pdf.

Research assistants

The team working on a project at the Commission almost invariably includes at least one research assistant (RA). RAs work in that capacity for, usually, a maximum of two years. Each recruitment round is highly competitive: in January 2017 we received 309 applications for 14 posts. Many RAs go on to build highly successful careers as barristers, solicitors or legal academics. The RAs who left us in 2017 went on to the following employers or pupillages among others: 7 Bedford Row; 39 Essex Chambers; Fountain Court Chambers; Goldsmith Chambers; 9 Gough Square; 4 Kings Bench Walk; 4 New Square; the Healthcare Professions Council; the Office of Parliamentary Counsel; Stockport District Council; and the staff of the Canadian Senate. Stephen Lewis and Professor Nick Hopkins each worked at the Commission early in their careers.

Consultation – protection of official data

Consultation is a key aspect of our working methods. The level of response to our consultation papers varies from low if the subject is highly technical to very high if it is of wide public interest. The most striking recent example is our consultation paper on the Protection of Official Data, published on 1 February 2017. This attracted a torrent of instant comment, followed by over 1,200 responses to the consultation. Some of the criticism was based on misconceptions – for example, that we were proposing to abolish a public interest defence under the Official Secrets Acts (no such defence has existed to date), or that we were proposing that anyone who publishes a leak about any aspect of Government policy should be liable to be sent to prison for 14 years (we were not). But many of the responses to the consultation paper were detailed, thoughtful and persuasive, and deserve very serious consideration. Our work on this difficult and contentious subject has highlighted the importance of consultation in the process of law reform.

Recent events

On 26 June 2017, after the end of the reporting year, the Lord Chief Justice of England and Wales, the Rt Hon Lord Thomas of Cwmgiedd, delivered the Law Commission's sixth Scarman Lecture, "'Law Reform Now' in 21st Century Britain – Brexit and Beyond".[5] He argued that the Law Commission "should be used to bring its great technical and legal expertise to assist in legislating for Brexit where appropriate in areas which are more technical than political, but nonetheless of the greatest importance to the State". He also noted that commercial law needs to be kept up to date; that legislative change is likely to be needed to deal with new forms of contract such as blockchain and smart contracts; and that consideration should be given to whether the Law Commission should be charged with ensuring that UK legislation meets the radical changes in the law which the digital revolution is likely to bring about. These topics will, I hope, be the subject of discussions between the Commission and the Government. We stand ready to assist if we can.

I conclude by again thanking my colleagues and the staff of the Law Commission who, despite operating in particularly uncertain times and under significant budgetary pressure, approach the important task of law reform with hard work, enthusiasm and diligence.

Sir David Bean

Chair

5 https://www.judiciary.gov.uk/wp-content/uploads/2017/06/lcj-speech-scarman-lecture-20170626.pdf.

Chief Executive's comment

As I complete my first full year as Chief Executive, this annual report provides me with an opportunity to reflect on some of the issues affecting the Law Commission.

Our people

First, I would like to echo our Chair's comments about our staff. I have been incredibly impressed with the hard work and expertise of everyone at the Commission. We are extremely fortunate to attract such a high quality team and I am grateful to everyone for their efforts this year. As with most of Government, we are being asked to do more with less and I know that the Commission must rise to this challenge. It is, however, a balance and I am keen to do all I can to make the Commission the type of place people want to work.

With that in mind, we have focused a great deal of attention on addressing some of the concerns raised in the annual People Survey. Although the Commission did well when compared to other parts of the Civil Service, we saw a disappointing dip, especially in relation to (1) leadership and managing change, (2) learning and development and (3) inclusion and fair treatment. To help combat some of these concerns, we have undertaken a number of activities. These range from creating our own learning and development policy to more regular engagement through regular all staff CEO updates and encouraging the development of cohort groups at the lawyer and research assistant grades. I am grateful to everyone for their support of this work and hope that we have created a more positive and inclusive environment as a result.

Our budget

We continue to operate within our Spending Review settlement, which equated to a 33% reduction across the four-year period to March 2020 and a 53% reduction overall since 2010-11. This has involved difficult decisions, including significant reductions in non-legal roles. As a general principle, I have sought to protect what I regard as our frontline – our lawyers, research assistants, economist and Parliamentary Counsel.

Any reduction of staff in these areas serves to reduce our capacity to undertake existing law reform projects, respond to Government priorities as well as to attract new work, even if project-specific funding is available. This in turn reduces our ability to earn income, thus completing a vicious circle. On the basis that almost all of our budget is comprised of staff cost, options open to the Commission to make more savings are therefore extremely limited. I firmly believe we have now reached the irreducible minimum.

Our work

The 13th Programme of Law Reform has been an excellent example of public consultation and one which served its purpose of developing a wide range of ideas for potential law reform projects. The scale of responses was unprecedented and, in my view, highlights the ongoing need for, and support for, the Commission. The difficult task has been to refine all of these ideas into a list of projects where, as the 2010 Protocol demands, the Government has a serious intention to take forward law reform.

We are operating in a very uncertain environment following the vote to leave the EU and snap election. This has caused delay which has directly affected our ability to secure projects and, in consequence, generate the additional specific funding that is now required to balance our budget. We are hopeful of gaining agreement of the 13th Programme before Christmas. I am confident it will contain a diverse and highly relevant range of projects.

Governance

The MoJ continue to act as our sponsor department. I am grateful to the MoJ team for developing a more proportionate governance mechanism which reflects the relatively low risk posed by the Commission in terms of impacting adversely on the department's objectives. This new level of oversight has helped us to focus our attention on the key issues whilst reducing the burdens placed on both organisations. It is a welcome development.

More generally, I continue to encourage the MoJ to think more strategically in terms of helping us to identify and respond to the priorities of wider Government. The 13th Programme process has, in my view, demonstrated a rather ad hoc approach which means it has been difficult for the Commission to direct its energies to those areas where our expertise could be of most benefit. As the Chair has said, there is an opportunity for the Commission to undertake law reform work in consequence of Brexit, but also other priorities which Government itself may not have the resource to undertake. MoJ can, I hope, be a strong voice for the Commission in securing appropriate work in the coming years.

Phillip Golding

Chief Executive

Part One:
Who we are and what we do

The Law Commission

The Law Commission is headed by five Commissioners, all of whom are appointed by the Lord Chancellor. At 31 March 2017, the Law Commissioners were:

- The Rt Hon Lord Justice Bean[6], Chair.
- Professor Nick Hopkins[7], Property, Family and Trust Law.
- Stephen Lewis[8], Commercial and Common Law.
- Professor David Ormerod QC[9], Criminal Law.
- Nicholas Paines QC[10], Public Law and Welsh Law.

The Commissioners are supported by the staff of the Law Commission. The staff are civil servants and are led by a Chief Executive.

The Law Commission was created by the Law Commissions Act 1965 for the purpose of reforming the law of England and Wales. It is a statutory public body, which is sponsored by the MoJ.

The Law Commission's principal objective is to promote the reform of the law. We do this by reviewing areas of the law and making recommendations for change. We seek to ensure that the law is as simple, accessible, fair, modern and cost-effective as possible.

A number of specific types of reform are covered by the Law Commissions Act 1965:

- Simplification and modernisation of the law.
- Codification.
- Removal of anomalies.
- Repeal of obsolete and unnecessary enactments.
- Consolidation of legislation.

We approach this work in two distinct strands: programmes of law reform and statute law work, which includes both statute law repeals and consolidation.

The progress we have made during 2016-17 in these areas of work is recorded in Part Two.

LAW COMMISSION BOARD

The Chair, four Commissioners, Chief Executive and non-executive board members meet as the Law Commission Board on a monthly basis. They are joined by the Law Commission's team managers. Board meetings are used to set the Commission's strategic direction, review risk, discuss operational matters and review the financial position.

NON-EXECUTIVE BOARD MEMBERS

We were delighted to have appointed Bronwen Maddox as the Law Commission's second non-executive board member. Bronwen joins Sir David Bell as a non-executive advisor, appointed to provide a level of support, independent challenge and expertise to the Commission when it is meeting as a Board. Bronwen comments on her experiences at the Law Commission so far on page 12.

OUR OBJECTIVES

As an organisation, we have worked together to identify the characteristics to which the Law Commission should aspire:

- To be the authoritative voice on law reform.
- To make a difference through our law reform work.
- To be proactive in promoting the need for law reform in key areas and achieve "good law".
- To have a strong reputation in the UK and abroad for being effective in the delivery of law reform.

6 Sir David Bean joined the Commission on 1 August 2015.

7 Professor Nick Hopkins joined the Commission on 1 October 2015.

8 Stephen Lewis joined the Commission on 1 January 2015.

9 Professor David Ormerod QC joined the Commission on 1 September 2010.

10 Nicholas Paines QC joined the Commission on 18 November 2013.

- To attract the best talent and be an excellent place to work.

Our Business Plan[11] for 2016-17 identified four priority areas for action for the Law Commission:

- Law reform – to make a difference through law reform.
- External relations and reputation – to engage proactively with our stakeholders and respond to their feedback.
- Our people – to attract the best and continue to ensure the Law Commission is an excellent place to work.
- Finance and governance – to ensure decision making that is robust.

The commitments to meet these priorities can be found at Appendix C. The Law Commission published its Business Plan[12] for 2017-18 in July 2017.

OUR RELATIONSHIP WITH THE MINISTRY OF JUSTICE

In July 2015 we agreed a Framework Document with the MoJ,[13] which sets out the broad framework for the department's governance of the Commission and how the relationship between us and the MoJ should operate.

The document outlines the responsibilities of the MoJ sponsorship team in relation to the Commission. The sponsorship team is our primary contact with the MoJ. Its members act as an advocate for us within the Ministry and other Departments, and makes sure that we are aware of MoJ's views and any relevant departmental policies.

The Framework makes it clear that, while the sponsorship team has a role in monitoring the Commission's activities, it has "no involvement in the exercise of the Commissioners' judgment in relation to the exercise of their functions".

The frequency with which ministers of the MoJ and other departments will meet members of the Commission, and the scope of the Commission's relationship with Parliament are also set out in the Framework Document, albeit that, in recent times, these arrangements have tended to operate more flexibly. It details the Lord Chancellor's statutory duties in relation to the Commission and the direct relationship we have with Parliament through, for example, maintaining contacts with Parliamentarians and committee chairs, and giving evidence in relation to our functions or projects.

THE LAW COMMISSION IN WALES

2016-17 has seen further advances in relation to the Law Commission's work in Wales.

Working with the Welsh Government

The Wales Act 2014 brought into force amendments to the Law Commission Act 1965 to take account of Welsh devolution, instigating significant changes to our relationship with the Welsh Government and how we work with Welsh Ministers in relation to devolved matters.

The Act empowers us to give information and advice to Welsh ministers. In turn, this enables Welsh ministers to refer work directly to the Commission whereas, previously, referrals could be made only through the Wales Office. This is a very welcome development that will give the people of Wales a stronger voice in law reform.

The 2014 Act also:

- provides for a protocol[14] setting out the working relationship between the Law Commission and the Welsh Government; and
- requires Welsh ministers to report annually to the Assembly about the implementation of our reports relating to Welsh devolved matters.

11 https://s3-eu-west-2.amazonaws.com/lawcom-prod-storage-11jsxou24uy7q/uploads/2016/07/Business_Plan_2016-17.pdf.

12 https://s3-eu-west-2.amazonaws.com/lawcom-prod-storage-11jsxou24uy7q/uploads/2015/05/Final-Business-plan.pdf.

13 Framework Document: Ministry of Justice and the Law Commission for England and Wales (2015).

14 Protocol rhwng Gweinidogion Cymru a Comisiwn y Gyfraith/Protocol between the Welsh Ministers and the Law Commission (2015).

Reforming the law in Wales

Over the course of the 12th Programme of Law Reform we included, for the first time, two law reform projects that related to Wales only in our programme of law reform:

- The Form and Accessibility of the Law Applicable in Wales – now concluded with the majority of the recommendations accepted. See page 32 for more details.
- Planning Law in Wales – a major consultation setting out proposals for the simplification of planning law in Wales is due to be published shortly. See page 31 for more details.

We continue to keep the machinery already in place to provide law reform in Wales under review, making improvements where we can. We have also recently expanded the role of one of our commissioners, Nicholas Paines QC, to give him special responsibility for Welsh law. In 2017 Nicholas spoke about law reform in Wales at the Legal Wales conference in Swansea.

As part of our 13th Programme consultation, we held a consultation event at Cardiff University in September 2016. This event was attended by representatives of the legal profession, academia, and the private, public and third sectors in Wales. We received numerous consultation responses from Welsh consultees, including proposals for projects in devolved areas of the law. The Commission also suggested two projects relating exclusively to Wales. The Welsh Advisory Committee has considered the proposals received and provided valuable input, both in relation to the Wales-only projects and to the impact in Wales of other suggested projects.

We are grateful for the support and contributions we have received from our colleagues and stakeholders in Wales.

Welsh Advisory Committee

We are grateful to have been supported throughout this year by our Welsh Advisory Committee. We established the Committee in 2013 to advise us on the exercise of our statutory functions in relation to Wales, and to give the people of Wales a stronger voice in law reform.

Welsh Language Policy

We published our Welsh Language Policy[15] on 4 September 2017. This sets out our commitment to treating with parity all those Welsh-commissioned projects and those projects which are likely to have significant public interest in Wales. We now routinely publish appropriate project documents bilingually.

Measuring success

The implementation of our recommendations for reform is clearly an important indicator of the success of the Law Commission. This is covered in detail in Part Three of this report.

However, implementation does not fully demonstrate the breadth of our impact. In an effort to assess our impact and influence, we take note of instances when the Law Commission is cited in judgments or during business in the Houses of Parliament. In 2016, for example, the Commission was mentioned 77 times in judgments in England and Wales and our name appears 141 times in Hansard, the official report of Parliamentary proceedings.

Our work is also widely quoted in academic journals and the media, with over 1,500 references to the Law Commission across academic, trade, local and national media in 2017 alone. Some of these will be made in support of the Commission; some will not. At the very least these figures show that the we continue to engage the attention of people with an interest in the law and what can be achieved through its reform.

15 https://s3-eu-west-2.amazonaws.com/lawcom-prod-storage-11jsxou24uy7q/uploads/2015/06/LC-Welsh-Language-Policy.doc.

There are also many reasons why our recommendations for reform may not be implemented beyond being rejected by Government. This may include a lack of parliamentary time to debate our proposals or a change in Ministerial priorities. In fact, the Law Commission has produced 227 sets of law reform recommendations over more than 50 years – only 14% of our reports have been rejected in that time and, more recently, only three reports have been rejected in the last 15 years.

Bronwen Maddox, non-executive board member

Bronwen Maddox, Director of the Institute for Government, joined the Law Commission as our second non-executive board member in November 2016.

“I was delighted to join the Law Commission as a non-executive board member. I had been impressed with what the Commission had done in bringing about reform that, however technical it might sound, could make a vast difference to people's lives.

I started in the role at the end of 2016, hardly a quiet time as the implications of the referendum vote to leave the European Union were becoming clear in terms of the demands on Government and parliamentary time. As a non-executive, I contribute by commenting on the wider social context of proposed reforms, trends likely to shape society and law, the challenge for Government of implementing certain changes, the process of getting legislation through Parliament and the potential reaction to proposals.

I have been impressed by the rigour that the Commission brings to its deliberations, its consultation on proposed reforms, the willingness of team members to adapt their conclusions in the light of evidence – and the collegiate spirit of the teams themselves, often working under considerable pressure. As shown by work in the past year and the proposed 13th Programme, the Commission has chosen subjects that range right across the fabric of national life and smooth out aspects of past legislation that can cause unwanted effects and often, a lot of distress. The recommended reform of Bills of Sale is one example, protecting those who have turned to this often high cost form of credit (for example, raising a loan against an asset such as a vehicle) while removing unnecessary administrative burdens and costs on lenders. The project on Wills is another example.

Brexit itself is likely to present the Law Commission with opportunities. So is the digital revolution, where the Commission may soon look to begin a project.

There are two sorts of pressures on the Commission which should be of concern, however. The first stems from the pressure on parliamentary capacity given that Brexit has squeezed out much legislation from the timetable. It would be a pity if this severely constricted Parliament's ability to get the Law Commission's reforms through.

The second is the ratcheting down of its resources over the years and the need to support a higher proportion of its work through funding from Government departments which commission some projects. Inevitably, there are implications for its ability to generate projects independently, guided by what the Commissioners think is most important. It would be regrettable if this compromised the independence with which it is seen to speak.”

Part Two:
Review of our work in 2016-17

Commercial and common law

Commissioner: Stephen Lewis

19/04/2016	Insurable interest	Consultation opened	page 14
13/06/2016	Consumer prepayments on retailer insolvency	Report published	page 14
31/03/2017	Event fees in retirement properties	Report published	page 15
27/04/2017	Patents, trade marks and designs: unjustified threats	Royal Assent	page 16
21/06/2017	Pension funds and social investment	Report published	page 16
10/07/2017	From bills of sale to goods mortgages	Consultation opened	page 17

Insurable interest

At its simplest, the requirement for insurable interest means that, for a contract of insurance to be valid, the person taking out the insurance must stand to gain a benefit from the preservation of the subject matter of the insurance, or to suffer a disadvantage should it be lost or damaged. The Life Assurance Act 1774 and the Marine Insurance Act 1906 provide, for insurance contracts which are covered by those Acts, that absence of insurable interest renders the contract void and unenforceable.

We have been told that the current law, which is unclear in some respects, and antiquated and restrictive in others, has had the effect of inhibiting the insurance market's ability to write particular types of product for which there is demand. We, together with the Scottish Law Commission, are working to develop recommendations to simplify and update the law in this area, and draft a Bill to implement those proposals.

Responses to our consultations have shown strong support for retaining the principle of insurable interest, said to guard against moral hazard, protect insurers from invalid claims and distinguish insurance from gambling. Our most recent consultation, which included a draft Bill, set out proposals to clarify the concept of insurable interest in indemnity insurance and extend the concept for life and related insurances, such as health insurance. We proposed that archaic restrictions should be removed in order to allow people to insure the lives of their children, cohabitants or employees.

Our proposals are intended to be relatively permissive, to ensure that, broadly speaking, any legitimate insurance products that insurers want to sell and people wish to buy could be made available. Whether insurance is appropriate in any given circumstances should be left to the good sense of insurers, with regulatory intervention if necessary.

We will produce an updated draft Bill, which will be limited to life and life related insurance, for consultation when resources allow.

Consumer prepayments on retailer insolvency

This project considered whether greater protection is needed for consumers who lose deposits or gift vouchers when retailers or other service providers become insolvent.

On 13 June 2016, we published our report setting out recommendations which would improve consumers' position on insolvency. We recommended:

- Regulating Christmas clubs and similar savings schemes, the failure of which pose a particular risk to vulnerable consumers.
- Introducing a general power for Government to require prepayment protection in sectors which pose a particular risk to consumers.
- Giving consumers more information about obtaining a refund through their credit or debit card issuer.
- Making changes to the rules on when consumers acquire ownership of goods when buying them.
- Considering a limited change to the insolvency hierarchy, to give a preference to the most vulnerable category of prepaying consumers.

Consumers who have made prepayments do not always lose out when a business ceases trading, particularly where consumers have paid by credit or debit card. We made recommendations designed to ensure that that the protections available to consumers who have paid by credit or debit card are better known. However, our research found that it is often the most vulnerable consumers, frequently paying by cash, who suffer the most. We made a case for limited reforms to protect vulnerable consumers in the most serious cases. These included protecting all money paid towards "savings" schemes such as Christmas hamper clubs, and considering a limited change to the insolvency hierarchy for consumers who have no other protections available to them.

The Insolvency Service, working with insolvency practitioners and UK Cards Association, has taken steps to implement those of our recommendations which related to information about debit and credit card refunds. These recommendations increase the chance that consumers who have made a prepayment by credit or debit card will be aware that they may be able to recover lost money from their card issuer. The Government's response to other recommendations is awaited.

Event fees in retirement properties

Each year thousands of older people consider a move to specialist retirement properties. These homes are almost always sold on a leasehold rather than freehold basis. Many of these leases require the owner to pay a fee on certain events – such as sale, sub-letting or change of occupancy. We call these "event fees". In 2013, the Office of Fair Trading investigated the use of transfer fees (a type of event fee). They found that terms in leases imposing this type of event fee were potentially unfair. As a result, in 2014, the Department for Communities and Local Government asked us to investigate. Event fees are levied by the majority of developers of the 160,000 retirement properties in England and Wales.

On 31 March 2017, we published a report recommending a code of practice which:

- Limits the circumstances in which event fees may be charged and, in certain cases, the amount that can be charged.
- Imposes obligations on landlords to provide transparent information about event fees to consumers at an early stage of the purchase process, including an indication of how much the event fee is likely to be.

We recommended that this code of practice should be approved by the Secretary of State for the Department for Communities and Local Government and, once approved, should be supported by an amendment to the Consumer Rights Act 2015, which would allow the code of practice to be enforced by consumers.

Our recommended reforms address concerns that event fees are charged in unfair circumstances. They also ensure that consumers are provided with clear information about event fees at an early stage in the purchase process. This would enable consumers to make informed decisions about purchasing a retirement property, and to appreciate what that means for their future financial obligations.

The recommended reforms are also intended to reduce the uncertainty about the legal status of event fee terms. If such uncertainty is removed or reduced, there is likely to be significant increased investment in this sector, leading to more options for consumers as they grow older. The Government's interim response is awaited.

Patents, trade marks and designs: unjustified threats

Unjustified, or "groundless", threats to sue someone for the infringement of a patent, trade mark or design right can cause commercial and reputational harm. Customers of a competitor may be influenced by threats, and in order to avoid expensive litigation, retailers and stockists may simply drop the competitor's products from their shelves, even though they are not infringing. In the 1800s, a statutory cause of action for patents was introduced to enable those who had been damaged commercially by unjustified threats to sue the person making the threat. Over time, this was extended to cover threats to sue in respect of trade marks and designs. However, the law developed in a piecemeal fashion so that protection against unjustified threats became inconsistent between the rights.

In April 2014 we published a report recommending reforms to the threats provisions for patents, trade marks and designs.[16] We proposed changes that would produce a clear and consistent law of unjustified threats that distinguished between those threats made to protect valuable rights against the most damaging forms of infringement, and those misused to cause commercial damage. The reforms would support disputing parties in reaching a negotiated settlement so avoiding litigation. We also recommended that professional advisers acting on behalf of their clients should no longer face liability for making threats.

The recommendations were accepted by Government and the Intellectual Property (Unjustified Threats) Bill was introduced into the Lords on 19 May 2016. It was given its third reading in the House of Commons on 21 March 2017 and received Royal Assent on 27 April 2017. The Act came into force on 1 October 2017.

For more detail on the project see page 18.

Pension funds and social investment

Since auto-enrolment was brought in by the Government in 2012, the amount of money in defined contribution pension schemes has increased significantly. By 2030 it is expected to total some £1.68 trillion. This raises questions about how the new pension assets are to be invested and whether at least a proportion could be invested for the wider social good – combining social and financial objectives in order to "do well and do good at the same time".

Following a call for evidence and over 20 meetings with stakeholders, our research found that barriers to social investment by pension funds are, in most cases, structural and behavioural rather than legal or regulatory. In our report published on 21 June 2017, we identified steps which could be taken by Government, regulators and others to minimise these barriers, including:

- Amending the law so that pension funds have to report on their policies on evaluating social impact, considering members' ethical concerns and exercising stewardship powers.
- Issuing guidance about how schemes can manage illiquid investments in their funds, such as investment in infrastructure.
- Taking steps to address barriers to consolidation of defined contribution pension schemes so they are more able to invest in illiquid assets.
- Encouraging pension providers and the pensions industry to devise a set of standard terminology around social investment, to help pension savers understand where their money is going.

We currently await the Government's interim response, due in December 2017.

16 (2014) LC 346.

From bills of sale to goods mortgages

Bills of sale are a way in which individuals can use goods they already own as security for a loan. Our 2016 report on Bills of Sale recommended that the Victorian Bills of Sale Acts should be repealed and replaced with modern legislation that imposes fewer burdens on lenders and provides more protection for borrowers. In February 2017, the Treasury asked us to draft a new Goods Mortgages Bill to implement the majority of our recommendations. The Bill was announced in the Queen's Speech in June 2017.

Our report made recommendations intended to:

- Protect vulnerable borrowers who are struggling to repay so that lenders will usually have to obtain a court order to before repossessing goods from borrowers, and give eligible borrowers the right to hand over the secured goods to the lender in full and final satisfaction of their debt.
- Protect innocent private purchasers who buy vehicles or other goods without realising that they are subject to a security interest.
- Remove unnecessary restrictions on secured lending to more sophisticated borrowers, such as high net worth individuals and unincorporated businesses.
- Save costs imposed on lenders by unnecessarily complex formality and registration requirements.

On 10 July 2017, we opened a consultation on a draft Goods Mortgages Bill. We followed this by publishing a further draft on 22 September, together with a document setting out our response to our July 2017 consultation and an update on the changes we have made to the draft Bill since then. We intend to publish a final report with draft Bill by the end of 2017.

Intellectual Property (Unjustified Threats) Act 2017

Intellectual property rights (IPRs) can be some of the most valuable assets owned by businesses and individuals and the law provides remedies for those whose rights are infringed. A threat to take action against an infringer, however, can be abused to damage commercial rivals. For example, empty threats to sue for infringement made to a competitor's customers can cause significant economic damage by driving them away. Making unjustified threats is, in effect, a form of unfair competition.

Protection against this kind of behaviour was introduced in legislation as early as the 1880s, whereby a person affected by an unjustified threat could sue the threatener. Since then, the law has developed in a piecemeal and sometimes incoherent way, making it confusing and less effective. If threatened, it was not clear what someone could do about it. And parties in a dispute, who wanted to settle their differences, were wary of entering into negotiation in case one or the other was accused of making an unjustified threat. This led to a culture of "sue first – speak later".

Calls for reform from those affected by the situation grew until in 2012 we were asked by the Intellectual Property Office to review the current law with a view to its reform. The Intellectual Property (Unjustified Threats) Act 2017, which came into force on 1 October 2017, is the result of that work.

What did we propose?

After detailed research and analysis of the current law, and that of other countries dealing with similar problems, in 2013 we undertook a consultation exercise on our proposals for reform. Our objectives were:

(1) To produce a clear, consistent and equitable law of unjustified threats, in particular by introducing consistency between the law as it applies to patents, trade marks and designs.

(2) To strike an appropriate balance which allows rights holders to protect their valuable IPRs but not to misuse threats in order to distort competition or stifle innovation.

We published a consultation paper, held roundtables and individual meetings with those affected by the current law and set up a working group drawn from intellectual property professional bodies, lawyers and practitioners, rights owners, businesses and academia. Consultees were unanimous that reform was needed. The current law was criticised for being unsatisfactory and a recipe for confusion. Several pointed out that smaller businesses were particularly prejudiced as they were less likely to be able to afford specialist legal advice, were more wary of being caught up in litigation and therefore were more vulnerable to bullying by larger, better financed competitors. The model for reform preferred by consultees and stakeholders was to build upon the current law, retaining much of what was familiar but to make it consistent, coherent and more straightforward.

The 2017 Act

The Intellectual Property (Unjustified Threats) Bill was introduced in the Lords on 19 May 2016. The Bill then passed through Parliament using our special procedure for non-controversial Bills. The Bill was thoroughly scrutinised in the House of Lords by a Special Public Bill Committee, which called for evidence from witnesses who either gave oral evidence or made written submissions. In this case there were five live evidence sessions as well as written evidence. Following these sessions and clause-by-clause review, the Committee reported on the Bill which then proceeded in the same way as any other. It received Royal Assent on the day of the prorogation of Parliament on 27 April 2017.

The 2017 Act replaces the existing threats provisions for patents, trade marks and designs with new ones. In all main respects they are consistent with each other for all the rights. The inconsistencies in the old law were a major concern for stakeholders.

Vicki Salmon (Chartered Institute of Patent Attorneys), Sarah Whitehead (Intellectual Property Office), Mark Anderson (Chair of the Intellectual Property Law Committee, Law Society), and James Porter (Intellectual Property Office).

Members of the commercial and common law team.

Criminal law

Commissioner: Professor David Ormerod QC

05/09/2016	Misconduct in public office	Consultation opened	page 20
December 2016	Search warrants	Project commenced	page 20
01/02/2017	Criminal records disclosures: non-filterable offences	Report published	page 21
02/02/2017	Protection of official data	Consultation opened	page 21
26/07/2017	Sentencing Code	Consultation opened	page 21
31/01/2017	Firearms	Royal Assent	page 22

Misconduct in public office

Misconduct in public office is a common law offence: it is not defined in any statute. It carries a maximum sentence of life imprisonment. The offence requires that: a public officer acting as such; wilfully neglects to perform his or her duty and/or wilfully misconducts him or herself; to such a degree as to amount to an abuse of the public's trust in the office holder; without reasonable excuse or justification. The offence is widely considered to be ill-defined and has been subject to recent criticism by the Government, the Court of Appeal, the press and legal academics. The project is a review of the current law and will provide options for reform and modernisation.

As part of our consultation, opened on 5 September 2016, we proposed the creation of two criminal offences to replace MIPO: an offence criminalising a breach of duty causing or risking serious harm and an offence criminalising an abuse of position for the purpose of achieving a benefit or causing a detriment. The offences could be created together or separately. Our proposals were based on an analysis of the harms and wrongs underlying the current offence. We also propose ways to define public office more clearly and consistently. Finally, we sought consultees' views on additional reforms, such as a review of sexual offences and the specification of public office as an aggravating factor for the purposes of sentencing.

We are now in the process of analysing consultation responses and conducting further research on issues that have arisen from consultation. We aim to report in 2018.

Search warrants

A search warrant is an order of a court authorising a police officer or other official to enter a building or other place and search for articles specified in the warrant. The law is so complicated that there are frequent challenges to warrants or to the way warrants are executed. It is also questionable whether the law is working effectively where the material sought is stored in electronic form. We have been asked by the Home Office to identify and address problems with the law governing search warrants and to produce reforms which will clarify and rationalise the law.

The project began in December 2016 and we are currently in the research and evidence-gathering stage. We aim to publish a consultation paper early in 2018.

Criminal records disclosures: non-filterable offences

In July 2016 we were requested by the Home Office to review one specific aspect of the criminal records disclosure system, known as "filtering". The filtering system provides a framework which regulates when an individual has to disclose convictions and cautions even though they are "spent". Under the Rehabilitation of Offenders Act 1974, a criminal conviction may become "spent" after a certain period of time. At that point the person is treated for most purposes as not having committed the offence. The scheme was introduced so that an individual who would otherwise be required to disclose all of his or her criminal offending history for certain purposes would not be required to do so if the convictions were for old and minor offences.

We published our report on 1 February 2017 making recommendations to:

- Simplify the existing legislative framework and introduce a number of technical reforms that will enable the filtering scheme to produce more accurate results.
- Conduct a wider review of the entire criminal records disclosure system and the provisions of the Rehabilitation of Offenders Act 1974 to ensure that the competing policy concerns of safeguarding and rehabilitation are appropriately balanced and that the disclosure system applies in a proportionate manner.

Our recommendations will reduce the likelihood of error in the criminal records disclosure system and enable users of the system to know what will and will not be disclosed on a criminal record certificate. They will also help reduce the number of legal challenges being brought with respect to the disclosure system and ensure that English law is compatible with the European Convention of Human Rights (ECHR). The report could substantially improve the disclosure system by ensuring that disclosures are directly relevant to the purpose behind the disclosure request.

Protection of official data

We were asked by the Cabinet Office to undertake an independent review of the law concerning the protection of official data, including the Official Secrets Acts, to ensure that the relevant statutes keep pace with the challenges of the 21st century. Our terms of reference asked us to consider the extent to which the relevant legislation effectively protects official information. Whilst this has been our focus, we have also sought to assess the extent to which the legislation strikes an appropriate balance between transparency and secrecy. Given that the relevant legislation was enacted long before the Human Rights Act 1998 came into force, we have also sought to assess the extent to which the relevant provisions comply with the ECHR.

On 2 February 2017, we launched a consultation seeking views on our suggestions to improve the law concerning the protection of official information. We published a number of provisional proposals on how the legislation could be improved in a way we believe will enhance the protection that is currently afforded to official information.

The consultation was originally planned for two months, but was extended to three months because of the large number of responses. We have continued to accept consultation responses beyond this period, and continue to engage with external consultees through meetings with practitioners as well as academic and media roundtables. We are now analysing consultation responses and aim to report by September 2018.

Sentencing Code

The law on sentencing is applied in hundreds of thousands of trials each year. Currently, the law lacks coherence and clarity. It is spread across many statutes, is frequently updated and has a variety of transitional arrangements. This makes it difficult for courts and practitioners to understand the present law governing the sentencing procedure. The Law Commission hopes to bring much needed clarity and simplicity to this area of law by introducing a single sentencing statute that will act as the comprehensive source of sentencing procedure law – the "Sentencing Code".

On 27 July 2017 we published our draft Sentencing Code Bill and an accompanying consultation paper. Over the last three years, working alongside the Office of the Parliamentary Counsel, we have produced a Bill consolidating sentencing procedure law. The consultation paper asks a number of questions concerning the decisions taken in the drafting of this Bill, as well as asking consultees for their thoughts on further proposed technical changes to the law. It also asks consultees to examine the draft Sentencing Code to ensure that the consolidation accurately reflects the current law subject to the technical amendments necessary to facilitate the consolidation.

For more detail on the project see page 24.

Firearms

In December 2015, we published our report on Firearms making recommendations to ensure that the law maximises public safety and secondly, to ensure that those who must both enforce and comply with the law know where they stand.

As we noted in our previous annual report, the current law relating to firearms creates significant practical difficulties for investigating authorities and prosecutors. It also makes it difficult for legitimate firearms users – such as hunting and shooting enthusiasts – to comply with the law. We made a number of recommendations intended to remedy the most pressing problems with the law on firearms. For example, ensuring that key terms, such as "firearm", are defined in unequivocal terms. The recommendations also minimise the risk of types of antique firearm that pose a risk to public safety being freely purchased.

On 31 January 2017, the Policing and Crime Act 2017 received Royal Assent. Part 6 of the Act implements the recommendations of our Firearms Report that was published at the end of 2015. The Act included the following provisions, which came into force on 2 May 2017:

- Section 125 – meaning of "firearm" and "component part" and an exception for airsoft guns.
- Section 127 – possession of articles for conversion of imitation firearms.
- Section 128 – controls on defectively deactivated weapons.
- Section 129 – controls on ammunition which expand on impact.
- Section 130 – authorised lending and possession of firearms for hunting etc.

The following provisions were also included and the aim is to implement these later:

- Section 126 – Firearms Act 1968: meaning of "antique firearm".
- Section 131 – limited extension of firearms certificates etc.
- Section 132 – applications under the Firearms Acts: fees.

As a result the law is now clearer and easier to use for investigators, prosecutors and those who legitimately use and own firearms and takes account of the technological developments that have taken place since the Firearms Acts were enacted.

Sentencing code

Lyndon Harris, the lead lawyer on the Sentencing Code project at an open public consultation event.

The law governing sentencing procedure is not working. It is contained in very many statutes spanning 700 years and is drafted in inconsistent and outdated language. Furthermore, there are layers upon layers of sentencing legislation which have been repealed but partially saved for historic cases. The result is an incoherent legislative scheme, in which the relevant law is both hard to find and difficult to apply. Inevitably, this causes errors of law, delays to other cases and unnecessary expense. We have set about bringing fundamental change to the area of sentencing procedure.

Sentencing is an extremely important part of the criminal justice process. It serves a crucial communicative function not only in holding accountable an individual who has broken the criminal law, but also in communicating to the public that such behaviour is not tolerated and that the individual responsible has been punished. Last year, 1.2 million offenders were sentenced in the criminal courts in England and Wales, with penalties ranging from fines through to life imprisonment. Sentencing serves many important purposes such as rehabilitation, public protection and punishment.

As such, the public want and expect clarity and transparency when the courts sentence offenders. However, there is near-universal agreement that the law of sentencing procedure lacks clarity, coherence, consistency and transparency. Judges have described sentencing law as "hell" and an "impenetrable thicket". A survey of 400 Court of Appeal (Criminal Division) cases from 2012 by the sentencing expert Robert Banks found that 262 were appeals against sentences and that in 95 of these cases unlawful sentences were passed in the Crown Court. These were not cases in which there was a disagreement as to what the level of sentence should be; these were cases where the basis for the sentence was wrong in law.

Such is the complexity and diffuse nature of the law of sentencing that judges face an increasingly difficult task when sentencing offenders. One stark example is that of the former Solicitor General, Sir Edward Garnier QC MP who also sat as a part time judge. Sir Edward stated that sentencing procedure had become so complex that he had decided not to sit in the criminal courts because he could not be sure that he was able to get the law right.

Our project, which was launched on 26 January 2015, received widespread support.

> A valuable and long-overdue stepping stone in the process of the rationalisation and clarification of the criminal law… [promising] clear benefits in terms of increasing efficiency and improving clarity and transparency of the sentencing process for offenders and the general public.
>
> The Rt Hon the Lord Thomas of Cwmgiedd, Lord Chief Justice of England and Wales.

The project began with the aim of creating a single statute containing the law on sentencing procedure. It had, and continues to have, the support of the judiciary, the legal professions and the Sentencing Council.

The first task in the project was to consult on what the law of sentencing procedure now is (Interim Report, October 2015). We created a four-volume, 1,300 page compilation of the current law and asked consultees whether we had accurately identified the law, and whether there were provisions included which ought not to be, or whether there were provisions not included which ought to be. Aside from some minor amendments, consultees agreed that we had accurately identified the law. That provided the foundation for the redrafting.

We also consulted separately on an aspect of the Sentencing Code which we considered would make the law significantly clearer and more transparent and result in cost savings by reducing delays and errors. This was our "clean sweep" policy: judges should be able to apply the codified law of sentencing procedure to all cases irrespective of the date of offending while still respecting fundamental rights of offenders, such as not imposing upon them a more severe penalty than that which was applicable at the time of the offence. We conducted a consultation exercise having published an issues paper setting out our provisional proposals. The paper suggested a drafting device to achieve our aim which would in effect 'clear the decks' by fully repealing all sentencing legislation which had been repealed but saved for historic cases, and fully commencing provisions which had been commenced prospectively only. There was widespread support for this policy and we produced a report in May 2016 (LC 365).

We subsequently worked with Parliamentary Counsel for 18 months on re-drafting the law to make it clearer and simpler and to correct any errors. We conducted a series of pre-consultation meetings with key stakeholders in order to inform our initial decisions on the structure of the new Code. In July 2017, we published a draft Bill and consultation paper (CP 232) which is open to consultation for a period of six months.

During the consultation period we are conducting a number of public events designed to raise awareness of the project, encourage engagement and answer questions about some of the more detailed issues raised by the project. The team is conducting expert roundtable discussions with judges, practitioners and academics, as well as consultation events across Crown Courts and Universities in England and Wales including in Birmingham, Leeds, London, Manchester, Cardiff and Bristol. After consultation closes in January 2018, we will analyse the responses, make any necessary amendments to the draft Bill and produce a final report in Summer 2018.

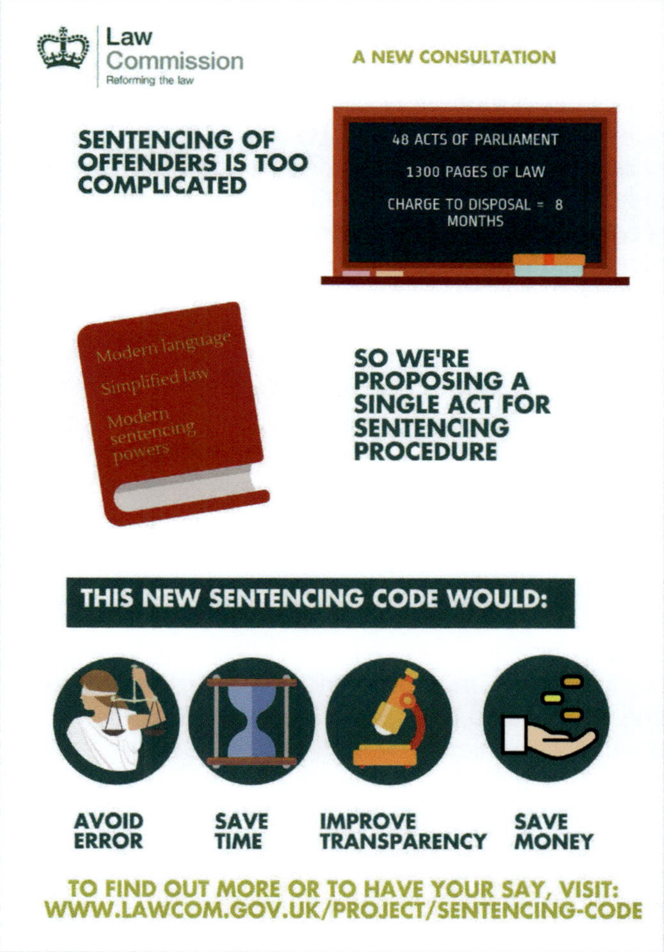

Property, family and trust law

Commissioner: Professor Nick Hopkins

15/12/2016	Enforcement of family financial orders	Report published	page 26
31/03/2016	Land registration	Consultation opened	page 26
13/07/2017	Wills	Consultation opened	page 27
14/09/2017	Technical issues in charity law	Report published	page 27

Enforcement of family financial orders

Each year thousands of separating couples apply to the courts for financial orders. Sometimes these orders are not complied with. The law of enforcement of family financial orders is a complicated area, contained in a range of legislation and court rules. Consequently, it can be difficult for parties, particularly litigants in person, to recover the money they are owed. The aim of the project was to make recommendations suggesting how this difficult area of law could be made more effective, efficient and accessible, and to strike a fairer balance between the interests of both parties.

We published our report on 15 December 2016, recommending the consolidation of all procedural rules dealing with the enforcement of family financial orders; the creation of a "route map" for enforcement proceedings, in the form of an Enforcement Practice Direction; and the provision of comprehensive guidance for litigants in person. We recommend changes to the enforcement procedure to ensure early disclosure of the financial circumstances of the debtor so that an appropriate method of enforcement can be selected, with provision for the court to obtain information from third parties (Government departments and private bodies). The report also recommends reforms to bring more of the debtor's assets, including those held in pensions and in joint bank accounts, within the scope of enforcement proceedings. Where debtors can, but will not, pay the report recommends new powers to disqualify debtors from driving, or to prevent them travelling abroad, in order to apply pressure to pay.

Our recommendations could result in creditors recovering additional funds of £7.5 million to £10 million each year, while debtors who cannot pay would be protected from undue hardship. The burden on the state would be reduced by making savings on welfare benefits. More widely, the benefits would include savings in court time; an increase in parties' access to and understanding of effective enforcement; and an increase in public confidence in the justice system.

Land registration

The land registration regime is of enormous and growing in importance. Approximately 84% of land in England and Wales is registered, with HM Land Registry maintaining nearly 25 million titles. Dealings and disputes that engage the land registration regime can be complex and require expert advice. Uncertainty in the regime makes advising clients difficult, incentivises litigation and increases costs for landowners.

We are currently undertaking a wide-ranging review of the Land Registration Act 2002, with a view to amending the parts that could be improved in light of the experience of its operation. In particular, we are examining the extent of HM Land Registry's guarantee of title, rectification and alteration of the register, and the impact of fraud. We are also re-examining the legal framework for electronic conveyancing.

Evidence suggests that some areas of the current law would benefit from revision or clarification. Our consultation, which ran from 31 March to 30 June 2016 revealed a range of often highly technical issues that have important implications for those who own land (whether the land is a home, a business or an investment), those with an interest in land (including mortgage providers), and HM Land Registry.

We published a consultation paper in March 2016 and aim to publish our final report and draft Bill in early Summer 2018.

Wills

The law of wills is largely a product of the 19th century, with the main statute being the Wills Act 1837. The law that specifies when a person has the capacity to make a will ("testamentary capacity") is set out in the 1870 case of Banks v Goodfellow. Our work on wills considers testamentary capacity; the rules that govern when a will is valid (such as requirements for signing and witnessing), and what happens when those rules are not properly followed; protecting vulnerable testators; and making wills electronically.

We published a consultation paper in July 2017 outlining our provisional proposals in respect of formality rules, a new mental capacity test which takes into account the modern understanding of conditions like dementia, and a suggestion that the age for making a will should be lowered from 18 to 16. We also want to pave the way for the introduction of electronic wills, to better reflect the modern world.

The proposed reforms will: support the more effective expression of people's testamentary freedom by ensuring that people's last wishes as to what should happen to their property are given effect; provide greater protection against fraud and undue influence for those making wills; and increase the clarity and certainty of the law. The changes potentially affect the entire adult population as most people can and should make a will. However, it is thought that 40% of adults do not, in fact, have a will and we hope that reform of the law will encourage those who do not have a will to make one.

Technical issues in charity law

There are about 167,000 charities registered with the Charity Commission and thousands more that are not required to register. Charities are a force for good and millions donate regularly to help them to help others. But there are problems with the law within which charities operate. This means that time and money is spent on administration when it could be used to further charitable causes. Our report, published on 14 September 2017, recommends reform of a range of technical issues within charity law.

The report recommends:

- That charities are given more flexibility to obtain tailored advice when they sell land, and that unnecessary administrative burdens are removed.
- Changes to the law to help charities amend their governing documents more easily, with Charity Commission oversight where appropriate.
- Increased flexibility for charities to use their permanent endowment, with checks in place to ensure its protection in the long term.
- Removing legal barriers to charities merging, when a merger is in their best interests.
- Giving trustees advance assurance that litigation costs in the Charity Tribunal can be paid from the charity's funds.
- Wider and rationalised powers for the Charity Commission including introducing a single set of criteria to decide changes to a charity's purposes; increased powers to prevent charities using misleading names; and the ability to confirm that trustees were properly appointed.

These recommendations will remove unnecessary administrative and financial burdens faced by charities as a result of inappropriate regulation and inefficient law, while safeguarding the public interest in ensuring that charities are run effectively. The reforms will save charities a large amount of time, as well as money. Those costs savings include an estimated £2.8 million per year from increased flexibility concerning sales of land.

For more detail on the project, see page 28.

Charity law reform

Our charity law report, published on 14 September 2017, recommends reform to address various technical legal issues in charity law. Whilst technical, these issues are important and have very practical consequences for charities. Shortly after completing his 2012 review of the Charities Act 2006, Lord Hodgson likened regulatory burdens on charities to the barnacles that slow down a ship:

> Each barnacle has very little effect. Trying to chip off one barnacle leaves one open to the accusation that one is either obsessive, irresponsible or lacking in judgment as to the use of parliamentary time, or possibly all three at once. In consequence, if one is tempted to leave all the barnacles in place, eventually the ship slows down.

Uncertainties in the law and unnecessary regulation can delay or prevent charities' activities, discourage people from volunteering to become trustees, and force charities to obtain expensive advice. A clear legal framework is essential for the Charity Commission and charities to work effectively, which in turn strengthens public trust and confidence in charities.

Our report is accompanied by a draft Bill, which would give effect to our recommendations. Many Law Commission reports are published with draft Bills, which are the product of joint working between our legal teams and our in-house Parliamentary Counsel, the legislative drafters who are seconded to the Commission from the Office of the Parliamentary Counsel.

We had decided questions of policy ("How should the law be reformed?") following our public consultations. Our final recommendations for reform had been devised from the incredibly detailed and helpful responses we had received to our consultation papers. Bill-drafting followed on from that, and is the process of translating the policy into the words of statute.

In preparing our draft Bill, we were seeking to produce legislation that would work in practice, without creating new uncertainties and difficulties in the process. We were also conscious of the need for the Bill to work for a diverse charity sector. We therefore sought feedback on an early draft of the Bill from a range of interested stakeholders.

We did not seek further views on questions of policy at this stage. Rather, we asked for comments on the technical operation of the clauses in the draft Bill:

- Do you understand them?
- Do they work?
- Will they cause practical problems?
- Can you foresee any unintended consequences?

We sought comments from key stakeholders (the Charity Law Association, our consultants at Veale Wasborough Vizards LLP and Judge Alison McKenna, Principal Judge of the First-Tier Tribunal) and officials from various Government bodies (the Charity Commission, the Privy Council Office, the Attorney General's Office, HM Land Registry, the Department for Digital, Culture, Media and Sport, the Department for the Environment, Food and Rural Affairs, and the Ministry of Justice).

After collecting extensive written comments on the draft Bill and attending meetings to discuss those comments, we worked through each comment with Parliamentary Counsel, assessing whether the clauses of the Bill should be amended, or whether the point should be addressed in some other way. We are very grateful to everyone who provided comments on the draft Bill.

Through this process of seeking comments on the practical workability of the draft Bill, we are confident both that the draft Bill has been improved and that – if implemented – its operation will be more easily understood in practice.

---

17 Trusts (Capital and Income) Bill, Report of the Special Public Bill Committee (2012-13) HL 42, p 50.

> Today's report from the Law Commission is important. Although its recommendations may appear to be highly technical, cumulatively I believe they would have a huge impact on the sector, helping trustees to work effectively in modern-day conditions.

Lord Hodgson, on the publication of our report.

We now await Government's response to our recommendations. If they are accepted, our draft Bill has been thoroughly scrutinised and is ready-and-waiting for implementation.

> As the Law Commission's report today notes, its recommendations are technical but important, with real practical consequences for charities. It offers a real opportunity to remove some of the complexity and inconsistencies which can make charity law difficult both to apply and to regulate.
>
> I hope the Government will now bring forward the draft Bill to implement some much needed reform.

Nicola Evans, Charities Counsel.

Public law and Welsh law

Commissioner: Nicholas Paines QC

04/02/2016	Electoral law	Interim report published	page 30
29/06/2016	Form and accessibility of the law applicable in Wales	Report published	page 30
30/06/2016	Planning law in Wales	Consultation opened	page 31
13/03/2017	Mental capacity and deprivation of liberty	Report published	page 31

Electoral law

Electoral law in the UK has grown complex, voluminous, and fragmented, with many statutes and secondary legislation governing a long list of elections and referendums. The twin aims of the project are to ensure, first, that electoral laws are presented within a rational, modern legislative framework, governing all elections and referendums; and second, that the law governing the conduct of elections and referendums is modern, simple and fit for purpose.

The central thrust of the reform is to simplify and modernise electoral law. We recommend a move from the current "election-specific" legislative framework to a holistic legal governance structure. In other words, in so far as possible, a single, coherent set of laws and rules governing all elections. Under this approach, one Act of Parliament would govern the core structure for delivering polls within the UK Government's competence, supplemented by simplified secondary legislation.

Through 2016-17 we worked closely with the Cabinet Office and the Electoral Commission to formulate a package of reforms which could be implemented by secondary legislation and which would provide practical assistance to stakeholders. We hope to report on this project in 2018.

Form and accessibility of the law applicable in Wales

The law across the UK can be difficult for professionals and the public to find and understand. In Wales, the process of devolution has made things even more complicated. It can be very difficult to access the law in devolved areas, in particular because of the pace at which significant areas of the law in Wales – such as education, health and housing – are diverging from the law in England.

In our report published on 29 June 2016, we recommended a new approach to law-making in Wales and ways to make the existing law applicable in Wales clearer, simpler and easier to access. Significant areas of the law in Wales should be codified. Legislation relating to areas such as education, housing, health and planning could be brought together into codes, creating one easily accessible piece of primary legislation to cover each subject. To keep codes intact, we recommend that amendments or future legislation should be made only by amending or adding to the code. We also recommend that secondary legislation should be re-enacted as amended.

The Counsel General sent the Welsh Government's final response to our report on 19 July 2017. We were pleased that the Welsh Government agreed or agreed in principle with the vast majority of our recommendations. The Welsh Government "agreed that a sustained, long term programme of consolidation and codification of Welsh law would deliver societal and economic benefits, and is necessary to ensure that the laws of Wales are easily accessible." A pilot project looking at "consolidation, codification and better publication" will run until early 2018.

For more detail on the project, see page 32.

Planning law in Wales

Planning law in Wales is unnecessarily complicated and, in places, difficult to understand. Planning legislation has not been consolidated since the Town and Country Planning Act 1990 and has, ever since, been supplemented by a succession of piecemeal changes. The increasing divergence between the law in England and Wales has made it doubly difficult to identify the planning law of Wales. We have been working with the Welsh Government to produce simplified planning laws for Wales.

We will be consulting on provisional proposals for technical reform. We are considering the following:

- The restatement of existing primary legislation so that, as far as reasonably practicable, it is contained within a single piece of legislation in a modern, consistent and well-ordered manner so as to be easily accessible to its readers.
- Adjustments to produce a satisfactory consolidated text – correcting errors, removing ambiguities and obsolete material, modernising language and resolving a variety of minor inconsistencies.
- The simplification of the law by streamlining and rationalising unnecessary process and procedure, but not introducing any substantial change of policy.
- Where appropriate, the writing into statute of propositions of law developed in case law where they might contribute towards more accessible and coherent legislation.

The consultation paper was due to be published in November 2017.

Mental capacity and deprivation of liberty

The Mental Capacity Act and the Deprivation of Liberty Safeguards (DoLS) aim to protect people who lack mental capacity, but who need to be deprived of liberty so they can be given care and treatment in a hospital or care home. In 2014, a House of Lords Select Committee concluded that the existing legislation is "not fit for purpose" and, at the same time, a decision of the United Kingdom Supreme Court had the effect of placing increasing burdens on local authorities and health and social care practitioners administering the DoLS. As a result, the Department of Health asked us to review the DoLS and make recommendations for their reform.

On 13 March 2017, we published our final report and draft Bill recommending that the DoLS be repealed and replaced urgently. The report sets out a replacement scheme for the DoLS – which we have called the Liberty Protection Safeguards.

Our reforms would improve the legal protections offered to people who lack capacity and are being detained for their care and treatment. They should deliver better, more proportionate protection and could result in a saving to the taxpayer, allowing the more efficient direction of resource to where it is most needed.

Government provided an interim response on 30 October 2017 acknowledging our work and noting that a final response should be expected in Spring 2018.

Form and accessibility of the law applicable in Wales

Legislation can be inaccessible everywhere in the UK, but the problem is accentuated in Wales by the evolving devolution settlement. Functions under many Acts of Parliament have been transferred to the Welsh ministers, but this is often not apparent in the original Act, giving the impression that power continues to lie with the Secretary of State. The picture is made more complicated by the pace at which significant areas of the law in Wales – such as education, health and housing – are diverging from the law in England.

Responding to our consultation paper on the matter, the Welsh Government set out the problem:

> For Welsh laws to be accessible it is essential that they are intelligible, clear and predictable in their effect. They must also be easily available. At least three factors militate against this aim. The first is the volume of legislation with its plethora of interconnecting and cross-referenced provisions, which at the moment create something of a patchwork of law. The second is the process of devolution itself, which can make legislation within the devolved areas more complex than would otherwise be the case. The third is the extent to which legislation in its updated form, in other words incorporating amendments made in new legislation to existing legislation, is freely available to the public and available in both of our official languages.

We held an extensive public consultation which was central to developing our understanding of the issues, and possible solutions. As part of the consultation process, we travelled throughout Wales attending or hosting some 50 consultation meetings. We held seminars at two Legal Wales conferences, and attended a discussion for third sector organisations hosted by the Wales Council for Voluntary Action.

We also spoke to and met a number of stakeholders including:

- Officials in the Welsh and UK Governments and the National Assembly.
- Assembly Members, legislative drafters, archivists, judges, lawyers and academics.

We received 47 detailed written responses to our consultation paper, and 28 responses to our questionnaire on the impact of inaccessibility. These responses helped to shape a number of measures designed to improve the accessibility of the law in Wales and guarantee it for the future. Our primary recommendation was that the Welsh Government aims to set out as much as possible of the law for which the Assembly has competence in a series of "codes", published in both English and Welsh.

The Counsel General sent the Welsh Government's final response to our recommendations on 19 July 2017, agreeing or agreeing in principle with the vast majority. Crucially the Welsh Government "agrees that a sustained, long term programme of consolidation and codification of Welsh law would deliver societal and economic benefits, and is necessary to ensure that the laws of Wales are easily accessible".

Members of the public and Welsh law team.

Statute law

Statute law

In 2015 we completed our examination of 20th century Acts and published our 20th Statute Law Repeals Report and Bill. The Bill still awaits introduction.

Part Three

Implementation of Law Commission law reform reports 2016-17

IMPLEMENTING LAW REFORM

Implementation of our reports is a crucial indicator of the extent to which we are meeting our statutory obligation, the "systematic development and reform" of the law. There have been a number of developments in recent years designed to increase the rate at which Law Commission reports are implemented:

- The Law Commission Act 2009, which places a requirement on the Lord Chancellor to report to Parliament annually on the Government's progress in implementing our reports. The Wales Act 2014 places a similar duty on Welsh ministers.
- Protocols between the Law Commission and Government, which sets out how we should work together.

LAW COMMISSION PARLIAMENTARY PROCEDURE

One further development is a dedicated Parliamentary procedure, approved by the House of Lords on 7 October 2010 as a means of improving the rate of implementation of Law Commission reports. Bills are suitable for this procedure if they are regarded as "uncontroversial".

Seven Law Commission Bills have now followed this procedure:

- Intellectual Property (Unjustified Threats) Act 2017.
- Insurance Act 2015.
- Inheritance and Trustees' Powers Act 2014.
- Trusts (Capital and Income) Act 2013.
- Consumer Insurance (Disclosure and Representations) Act 2012.
- Third Parties (Rights against Insurers) Act 2010.
- Perpetuities and Accumulations Act 2009.

IMPLEMENTATION OF OUR REPORTS 2016-17

Between 1 April 2016 and 30 October 2017 we published nine final reports with recommendations for law reform:

- Consumer Prepayments on Retailer Insolvency, 13 July 2016.
- Form and Accessibility of the Law Applicable in Wales, 29 June 2016.
- Bills of Sale, 12 September 2016.
- Enforcement of Family Financial Orders, 15 December 2016.
- Criminal Records Disclosures: Non-Filterable Offences, 1 February 2017.
- Mental Capacity and Deprivation of Liberty, 13 March 2017.
- Event Fees in Retirement Properties, 31 March 2017.
- Pension Funds and Social Investment, 21 June 2017.
- Charity Law – Technical Issues, 14 September 2017.

The statistics from the creation of the Commission in 1965 to 30 October 2017 are:

- Law reform reports published – 227.
- Implemented in whole or in part – 149 (66%).
- Accepted in whole or in part, awaiting implementation –9 (4%).
- Accepted in whole or in part, will not be implemented – 5 (2%).
- Awaiting response from Government – 23 (10%).
- Rejected 31 – (14%).
- Superseded – 10 (4%).

REPORTS IMPLEMENTED

Electronic Communications Code

- Digital Economy Act 2017.

The Electronic Communications Code is the statutory regime that governs relationships between landowners and communications operators when placing communications infrastructure on public and private land. This project focused on private property rights between landowners and electronic communications operators. It did not consider planning law.

In February 2013, we made recommendations[18] to form the basis of a revised code. The proposed changes to the code would set out the legal position in clear terms, provide the clarity that the current code lacks, and provide an efficient forum for dispute resolution.

The Government published details of its revised proposals for a new Electronic Communications Code on 17 May 2016. The proposed reforms remained broadly aligned with our recommendations, with some key exceptions. In particular, Government has decided to adopt a different basis for the valuation of code rights and to confer automatic rights to upgrade and share apparatus. Those proposed reforms were implemented in the Digital Economy Act 2017.

Firearms

- Policing and Crime Act 2017.

In our report published in December 2015[19], we made a number of recommendations to address perceived weaknesses in the law governing the possession and acquisition of firearms and to maximize public safety and improve the clarity of the law. The Home Secretary broadly accepted many of our recommendations and a number of legislative changes were introduced under the Policing and Crime Act 2017 which received Royal Assent on 31 January 2017.

For more information on this project see page 22.

Intellectual property (groundless threats)

- Intellectual Property (Unjustified Threats) Act 2017.

Intellectual property law has long-standing provisions which protect certain businesses from being harmed by unjustified threats. The current statutory provisions have been criticised for not working as well as they should. We published our final report in October 2015[20] with draft Bill text. The Government accepted our recommendations for change.

The Intellectual Property (Unjustified Threats) Bill was introduced into the House of Lords in May 2016 using the special procedure and it received Royal Assent on 27 April 2017.

For more information on the project see page 16.

Late payment of insurance claims

As part of our review of insurance contract law conducted jointly with the Scottish Law Commission, we considered the issue of late payment of insurance claims. We found that, where an insurer refused to pay a valid claim or paid it only after unreasonable delay, the existing law did not provide a remedy for the policyholder. Notably, the policyholder was not entitled to damages for any loss suffered as a result of the insurer's unreasonable actions.

In July 2014, we recommended reform of the law in this area. We recommended that there should be an implied term in every insurance contract requiring the insurer to pay valid claims within a reasonable time, with what constituted a "reasonable time" depending on the circumstances of the case. We said that breach of that term should give rise to contractual remedies, including damages, but that insurers should not be liable for delays caused by genuine disputes.

Our draft clauses were included in the Enterprise Act 2016, and now form part of the Insurance Act 2015. They extend to the whole of the UK and came into force on 4 May 2017.

18 (2013) LC 336.

19 (2015) LC 363.

20 (2015) LC 360.

REPORTS IN THE PROCESS OF BEING IMPLEMENTED

Fiduciary duties of investment intermediaries

We published our report on fiduciary duties of investment intermediaries in July 2014. The report explained the nature of fiduciary duties and other duties to act in the best interests of savers, and clarified how far those who invest on behalf of others may take account of factors such as social and environmental impacts and ethical standards. The report concludes that legislation on this issue is not required.

The Government published its response in October 2014, welcoming the findings and our clear guidance that trustees should not focus exclusively on maximizing short term goals.

Our report made a number of specific recommendations to Government departments, and to the Financial Conduct Authority (FCA) and the Pensions Regulator (TPR), aimed at embedding its findings in relevant regulations and guidance, and addressing other issues identified in the course of the review. These recommendations have been implemented in part.

Matrimonial property, needs and agreements

- Final report and draft Bill published 27 February 2014.[21]
- Interim response from Government 18 September 2014.

This project was set up, initially under the title "Marital Property Agreements" to examine the status and enforceability of agreements (commonly known as "pre-nups") made between spouses and civil partners (or those contemplating marriage or civil partnership) concerning their property and finances.

In February 2012 the scope of the project was extended to include a targeted review of two aspects of financial provision on divorce and dissolution, namely provision for the parties' financial needs and the treatment of non-matrimonial property.

We published our final report in February 2014, making the following recommendations:

- The meaning of "financial needs" should be clarified by the provision of guidance so that it can be applied consistently by the courts.
- Legislation be enacted introducing "qualifying nuptial agreements".
- Work should be done to assess whether a formula for calculating payments would be feasible, but only when sufficient data is available about divorce outcomes under the current law.

The Government's interim response was published on 18 September 2014. The Government has accepted and taken action on the recommendation for guidance. The Family Justice Council developed financial guidance for separating couples and unrepresented litigants, which it published in September 2015, followed by publication of guidance for the judiciary on financial needs in June 2016.

With regard to our recommendations on a financial tool for separating couples the Government has convened a research advisory group to explore the feasibility of developing such a tool. The Government is considering qualifying nuptial agreements as part of a wider consideration of options for further private family law reforms and will respond in due course.

21 (2014) LC 343.

REPORTS AWAITING IMPLEMENTATION

Bills of sale

- Report published 12 September 2016.[22]

In 2014, HM Treasury asked the Law Commission to review the Victorian-era Bills of Sale Acts. The Law Commission's recommendations were published in September 2016 recommending that the bills of sale legislation should be repealed in its entirety and replaced by a new Goods Mortgages Act. The Government agreed with the majority of our recommendations and we are now drafting a Bill which would implement those recommendations.

For more information on this project see page 17.

Easements, covenants and profits à prendre

- Final report and draft Bill published 8 June 2011.[23]

This project examined the general law governing:

- Easements – rights enjoyed by one landowner over the land of another, such as rights of way.
- Covenants – promises to do or not do something on one's own land, such as to mend a boundary fence or to refrain from using the land as anything other than a private residence.
- Profits à prendre – rights to take products of natural growth from land, such as rights to fish.

These rights are of great practical importance to landowners and can be fundamental to the use and enjoyment of property. We looked closely at the characteristics of these rights, how they are created, how they come to an end and how they can be modified.

Our report recommended reforms to modernise and simplify the law underpinning these rights, making it fit for the 21st century and a modern registration system.

The recommendations would remove anomalies, inconsistencies and complications in the current law, saving time and money by making it more accessible and easier to use for those who rely on and engage with these interests most: homeowners, businesses, mortgage lenders and those involved in the conveyancing process. They would give new legal tools to landowners to enable them to manage better their relationships with neighbours and facilitate land transactions. Furthermore, the reforms would give greater flexibility to developers when building estates where there would be multiple owners and users.

The Government announced in the Housing White Paper[24] published on 7 February 2017 that:

"The Government also intends to simplify the current restrictive covenant regime by implementing the Law Commission's recommendations for reform and will publish a draft Bill for consultation as announced in the Queen's Speech."

This supplemented the earlier announcement on 18 May 2016 that the Government intended to bring forward proposals in a draft Law of Property Bill to respond to the Commission's recommendations[25]. A draft Bill is being prepared for publication and we are assisting Government with its preparation.

22 (2016) LC 369.

23 (2011) LC 327.

24 https://www.gov.uk/government/uploads/system/uploads/attachment_data/file/590043/Fixing_our_broken_housing_market_-_housing_white_paper.pdf Annex A para 35.

25 https://www.gov.uk/government/publications/queens-speech-2016-background-briefing-notes page 61.

Level crossings

- Final report, with draft Bill and draft regulations published 25 September 2013.[26]

This joint report with the Scottish Law Commission seeks to improve the law relating to the 7,500 to 8,000 level crossings in Great Britain.

Our recommendations would:

- Create a new, more streamlined procedure to close individual level crossings where it is in the public interest to do so.
- Bring safety regulation entirely under the umbrella of the Health and Safety at Work etc. Act 1974, and provide tools to support this.
- Impose a statutory duty on railway and highway operators to consider the convenience of all users, and to co-operate with each other when carrying out their obligations in respect of level crossings.
- Provide clarity regarding the position of statutory level crossings.
- Disapply outdated or obsolete statutory provisions.

The Government provided a final response to the report in October 2014, accepting the majority of our recommendations.[27] The Department for Transport published an action plan in December 2014, setting out an indicative timetable for implementing our recommendations and identifying a number of areas where further consideration with stakeholders is needed before reaching a conclusion.

Public service ombudsman

- Final report published 14 July 2011.[28]

Our 2011 report focuses on five ombudsmen: the Parliamentary Commissioner; the Health Service Ombudsman; the Local Government Ombudsman; the Public Services Ombudsman for Wales; and the Housing Ombudsman.

The report makes a series of recommendations aimed at improving access to the public services ombudsmen, ensuring that they have the freedom to continue their valuable work and improving their independence and accountability. The report's key recommendation for a wider review has now taken place, which in turn has led to legislative reform to enable the creation of a single Public Service Ombudsman.

The Government published the draft Public Service Ombudsman Bill on 5 December 2016. If implemented, the draft Bill would abolish the present Parliamentary and Health Service Ombudsman and the Local Government Ombudsman and create a new organisation with strengthened governance and accountability. It would improve access to the ombudsman's services by allowing for all complaints to be made with or without the help of a representative and in a variety of formats to meet the digital age. The draft Bill was scrutinised by the Communities and Local Government Committee on 6 March 2017, with next steps still to be confirmed.

Regulation of health and social care professionals

- Final report and draft Bill published 2 April 2014.[29]

This project dealt with the professional regulatory structure relating to 32 health care professions throughout the UK, and social workers in England – more than 1.5 million professionals in total. It was the first ever tripartite project conducted jointly with the Scottish Law Commission and the Northern Ireland Law Commission.

Our final report and draft Bill set out a new single legal framework for the regulation of health and social

26 (2013) LC 339.
27 (2015) HC 1062.
28 (2011) LC 329.
29 (2014) LC 345.

care professionals and reforms the oversight role of Government in relation to the regulators.[30]

The Government published its response on 29 January 2015, noting the need for further work on refining our recommendations to achieve the priorities of better regulation, autonomy and cost-effectiveness while maintaining a clear focus on public protection.

On 31 October 2017 the Government published a consultation paper on reforming regulation which builds upon our report.

The Health and Social Care (Safety and Quality) Act 2015 implemented our recommendations that all regulatory bodies and the Professional Standards Authority have the consistent overarching objective of promoting public protection and that regulatory bodies have regard to this objective in fitness to practise proceedings.

Taxis

- Final report and draft Bill published 23 May 2014.[31]

This project was proposed as part of the 11th Programme by the Department for Transport. Its aim was to take a broadly deregulatory approach to the process of modernising and simplifying the regulatory structures for this important economic activity.

In May 2012 we published our consultation paper,[32] proposing a single statute to govern both the taxi and private hire trades, and the setting of national standards in order to free up the private hire market. The interest was such that we had to extend the consultation period twice. We received just over 3,000 responses, a then record number for any of our consultations.

Some of our proposals provoked a great deal of controversy. In April 2013 we published a short interim statement[33] explaining that we had changed our views on abolishing the ability of local licensing authorities to limit taxi numbers and refined our views in other areas. We also published all of the responses received.

Our report and draft Bill were published in May 2014. Although the Government has not yet responded formally to our recommendations, two taxi and private hire measures – based on our recommendations – were included in the Deregulation Act 2015, which received Royal Assent in March 2015. The Welsh Government has recently concluded a consultation on taxi and private hire vehicle licensing which is based heavily on our recommendations.

Wildlife

- Report on the control of invasive non-native species published February 2014.[34] Recommended reforms given effect in the Infrastructure Act 2015.
- Final report on remaining elements, with draft Bill, published 10 November 2015.[35]

Wildlife law is spread over numerous statutes and statutory instruments, dating back to the 19th century. The legislation is difficult for people and businesses to access, for policy makers to adapt and for everyone to understand.

This project, which was proposed by the Department for Environment, Food and Rural Affairs (Defra) and included in our 11th Programme, considered the transposition of key EU directives on wild birds and those animals and plants characterised as European Protected Species, and their integration with other, domestic, legal structures. It also sought to bring

30 Regulation of Health Care Professionals: Regulation of Social Care Professionals in England (2014) LC345/SLC237/NILC18.

31 (2014) LC347.

32 (2012) LCCP 203.

33 http://www.lawcom.gov.uk/project/taxi-and-private-hire-services/.

34 (2014) LC 342.

35 (2015) LC 362 (two volumes).

various purely domestic protection regimes for specific species into the same legislative structure.

In March 2012 the Government asked us to add consideration of the possibility of appeals against licensing decisions by regulatory bodies to the project.

We held a consultation in 2012 proposing a single statute bringing together most of the law relating to wildlife.[36] In addition to making specific proposals on the most appropriate way of transposing the EU directives, we also looked at the current regime for the enforcement of wildlife legislation, including both criminal offences and civil sanctions, and at appeals.

Following a request by Defra to bring forward one element of the project, we published a report on the control of invasive non-native species in February 2014.[37] Our recommendations in relation to species control orders were given effect in the Infrastructure Act 2015. Our final report and draft Bill on the remaining elements of the project were published in November 2015.[38]

The Government issued its response on 22 November 2016, explaining that exit from the EU provides an opportunity to re-examine our regulatory framework so that it meets our needs in future including our international obligations. The Government will therefore consider the implications of EU Exit on wildlife policy before deciding whether and how to implement our recommendations.

REPORTS AWAITING A GOVERNMENT DECISION

Cohabitation

Cohabitation: The Financial Consequences of Relationship Breakdown

- Final report published 31 July 2007.[39]
- Holding response from Government 6 September 2011.[40]

In this project, at the Government's request, we examined the financial hardship suffered by cohabitants or their children on the termination of cohabitants' relationships by breakdown or death. The existing law is a patchwork of legal rules, sometimes providing cohabitants with interests in their partners' property, sometimes not. The law is unsatisfactory: it is complex, uncertain and expensive to rely on. It gives rise to hardship for many cohabitants and, as a consequence, for their children.

Our report recommended the introduction of a new scheme of financial remedies that would lead to fairer outcomes on separation for cohabitants and their families.

The scheme is deliberately different from that which applies between spouses on divorce and, therefore, does not treat cohabitants as if they were married. It would apply only to cohabitants who had had a child together or who had lived together for a specified number of years (which the report suggests should be between two and five years).

In order to obtain financial support – which might be in the form of a cash lump sum or transfer of a property, but not ongoing maintenance – applicants would have to prove that they had made contributions to the relationship that had given rise to certain lasting financial consequences at the point of

36 (2012) LCCP 206.

37 (2014) LC 342.

38 (2015) LC 362 (two volumes).

39 (2007) LC 307.

40 Written Ministerial Statement, Hansard (HC), 6 September 2011, col 16WS.

separation. For example, one partner might have enjoyed an enhanced earning capacity because the other partner took on responsibility for childcare.

In broad terms, the scheme would seek to ensure that the financial pluses and minuses of the relationship were fairly shared between the couple. For example, if one partner were disadvantaged in the job market as a result of time spent bringing up the couple's children, they might receive some financial compensation from their former partner to support them while retraining or otherwise preparing to return to work.

The report recommended that there should be a way for couples, subject to necessary protections, to opt out of any such agreement, leaving them free to make their own financial arrangements.

In 2011 the Government announced that it did not intend to take forward our recommendations for reform during that Parliament. The Government will be considering the Commission's recommendations in the context of the further reforms to the family justice system currently under consideration.

Intestacy and Family Provisions Claims on Death (Cohabitants)

- Final report and draft Inheritance (Cohabitants) Bill published 13 December 2011.
- Holding response from Government 21 March 2013.[41]

In this project we examined two important aspects of the law of inheritance: the intestacy rules that determine the distribution of property where someone dies without a will; and the legislation that allows certain bereaved family members and dependants to apply to the court for family provision.

Our final report, Intestacy and Family Provision Claims on Death, was accompanied by two draft Bills to implement our recommendations.[42] The first Bill was implemented and became the Inheritance and Trustees' Powers Act 2014. The second Bill, the draft Inheritance (Cohabitants) Bill, would:

- Reform the law regarding an application for family provision by the survivor of a couple (who were not married or in a civil partnership) who had children together.
- In defined circumstances, entitle the deceased's surviving cohabitant to inherit under the intestacy rules where there was no surviving spouse or civil partner. Generally speaking, this entitlement would arise if the couple lived together for five years before the death or for two years if they had a child together.

The Government announced in March 2013 that it did not intend to implement the draft Inheritance (Cohabitants) Bill during the then-current Parliament. The Government will be considering the Commission's recommendations in the context of the further reforms to the family justice system currently under consideration.

Conservation covenants

- Final report and draft Bill published 24 June 2014.[43]
- Response from Government 28 January 2016.

Currently, landowners can agree to use or not to use their land in a particular way. But any agreement will be enforceable against future owners only if certain conditions are met: it must impose only restrictions (for example, not to build on the land), not positive obligations (for example, to maintain a dry stone wall); and those restrictions must "touch and concern" other land nearby by providing an identifiable benefit to that land. This limitation can make it difficult to pursue long-term conservation goals.

This project considered the case for permitting landowners to enter into long-lasting and enforceable agreements where a conservation objective would

41 Written Statement, Hansard (HL), 21 March 2013, vol 744, col 59WS.

42 (2011) LC 331.

43 (2014) LC 349.

be met by an obligation to use, or not use, land in a particular way. These types of agreements, which already exist in other jurisdictions such as the USA, Canada, Australia, New Zealand and Scotland, are not specifically linked to nearby land. They allow a landowner to agree, for example, to maintain a woodland habitat and allow public access to it, or to refrain from using certain chemicals on land.

The consultation for this project ran from March to June 2013 and we published our final report and draft Bill on 24 June 2014.[44] The report recommends the introduction of a new statutory scheme of conservation covenants in England and Wales. In this scheme, a conservation covenant would:

- Be formed by the agreement of two parties – a landowner (a person with a freehold estate or leasehold estate of more than seven years), and a responsible body drawn from a limited class of organisations.
- Be able to contain both restrictive and positive obligations.
- Be capable of binding the landowner's successors in title (that is, all subsequent owners) after he or she has disposed of the land.
- Be made for the public good.

The then Secretary of State for the Environment, Food and Rural Affairs (Rt Hon Elizabeth Truss MP) wrote to the Commission on 28 January 2016 praising the quality of our work and giving a commitment to explore the role conservation covenants could play in the 25-year Environment Plan being prepared by the department.

Consumer prepayments on retailer insolvency

- Final report published on 13 June 2016.
- Awaiting Government response.

The project considered whether greater protection is needed for consumers who lose deposits or gift vouchers when retailers or other service providers become insolvent.

We have been discussing our recommendations with the Department for Business, Energy and Industrial Strategy (BEIS) and await the formal Government response. More information on this project is available on page 14.

Contempt of court: court reporting

- Final report published 26 March 2014.[45]
- Holding response from Government 13 March 2015.[46]

This report aims to modernise the way court reporting restrictions are communicated to the media. Reporting restrictions can be imposed by the judge in a case where publication of certain information may prejudice a fair trial. Typically, the order will provide that publication should be postponed until after the trial (or any linked trial) has finished. If the media breach such an order they will be in contempt of court and liable to criminal penalties. Under current law these important orders are communicated to the media by printing a copy of the order and posting it on the door of the court. This makes it difficult for the media to find out whether a reporting restriction is in place, leading to increased risks of prejudicing a fair trial, as well as the media being sometimes overly cautious in reporting, to avoid the risk of being found to be in contempt. In the report we recommended:

- Introducing a publicly accessible database available on the internet (similar to the one that already operates in Scotland) listing the court hearings in which restrictions are currently in place.
- Creating a more extensive restricted database where, for a charge, registered users could find out the detail of the reporting restriction and could sign up for automated email alerts of new orders.

44 (2014) LC 349.

45 (2014) LC 344.

46 Report on the Implementation of Law Commission Proposals, Ministry of Justice (2015), paragraph 77.

These recommendations would greatly reduce the risk of contempt for publishers – from large media organisations to individual bloggers – and enable them to comply with the court's restrictions or report proceedings to the public with confidence. We also undertook a pilot study that demonstrated the likely efficiency of such a scheme.

The Government has welcomed our recommendations and stated its intention to respond formally when the Criminal Justice System Common Platform is implemented.

Criminal records disclosures: non-filterable offences

- Final report published 1 February 2017.
- Awaiting Government response.

In July 2016, we were asked by the Home Office to review one specific aspect of the criminal records disclosure system, known as "filtering".

On 1 February 2017, we published our report. Within the narrow confines of this project, the report includes a recommendation that a statutory instrument should set out a single, itemised list of non-filterable offences in the future. We recommended a wider review of the disclosure system and the Government is considering our recommendations.

More information on the project is available at page 21.

Data sharing between public bodies

- Scoping report published 11 July 2014.[47]
- Interim Government response received on 24 December 2014.

Public bodies frequently report difficulties in sharing data with other public bodies, to an extent that impairs their ability to perform their functions for citizens. Some of these problems stem from defects in the law itself, and some from problems with understanding the law.

We conducted this project as a scoping review designed to identify where the problems truly lie and what should be done to address them. We ran a consultation during Autumn 2013 and published our scoping report in July 2014.

In the report we concluded that a full law reform project should be carried out in order to create a principled and clear legal structure for data sharing.

The Government welcomed the publication of our scoping report and sent an interim response on 24 December 2014, which noted the usefulness of the scoping report and its resonance with the Government's work in the open policy making space. The open policy making process and subsequent public consultation identified a number of priority areas taken forward in the Digital Economy Act, which received Royal Assent on 27 April 2017.

Enforcement of family financial orders

- Final report published on 15 December 2016.
- Interim Government response received on 2 August 2017.

We published our report on enforcement of family financial orders in December 2016, following concerns raised by practitioners that the legal routes and procedures for enforcing payment of financial orders made by the family court were unnecessarily complex. For more information see page 26.

The Government provided an interim response to the Commission's recommendations on 2 August 2017, indicating that the report provided a firm basis for consideration of the full extent of the problem of the non-payment of family financial orders and the ways to tackle it. A full response will be provided after consideration of the report's recommendations in the context of the Government's broader thinking on the family justice system.

47 Data Sharing between Public Bodies: A Scoping Report (2014) LC 351.

Event fees in retirement homes

- Final report published 31 March 2017.[48]
- Awaiting Government response.

In March 2017, we published a report recommending reforms to address concerns that event fees are charged in unfair circumstances. They will also ensure that consumers are provided with clear information about event fees at an early stage in the purchase process. This will enable consumers to make informed decisions about purchasing a retirement property, and to appreciate what that means for their future financial obligations. For more information see page 15.

We are awaiting a response from the Government to these recommendations.

Hate crime

- Final report published 28 May 2014.[49]
- Awaiting Government response.

This project was referred to us by the MoJ following the publication of the Government's three-year Hate Crime Action Plan in March 2012. As part of our extensive consultation work we hosted a symposium with over 100 interested stakeholders and received over 150 responses to our consultation.

The police and Crown Prosecution Service record a crime as a "hate crime" if the victim or anyone else believes that it is motivated by hostility based on any one or more of five characteristics: (1) disability; (2) transgender identity; (3) race; (4) religion; and (5) sexual orientation. Currently, the substantive criminal law regarding hate crime falls under three Acts:

- The Crime and Disorder Act 1998 (which covers "aggravated offences" on grounds of race or religion).
- the Public Order Act 1986 (which covers stirring up hatred on grounds of race, religion or sexual orientation).
- Sections 145 and 146 of the Criminal Justice Act 2003 (which cover enhanced sentencing for offences motivated by hostility to any of the five protected characteristics).

The project examined the case for extending the aggravated offences and the offences of stirring up hatred to include all five of the protected characteristics. We also considered use of the current legislation around enhanced sentencing for hate crimes.

In our report we made the following key recommendations, that:

- The enhanced sentencing system for hate crimes be strengthened and that anyone given an enhanced sentence for hostility should have this recorded on the Police National Computer.
- The Sentencing Council should produce sentencing guidelines to deal with hate crime.
- There should be a full-scale review of aggravated offences or, in the absence of this, the extension of aggravated offences to include disability, sexual orientation and transgender identity.
- The stirring up offences should not be extended.

We are awaiting a response from the Government to these recommendations.

The High Court's jurisdiction in relation to criminal proceedings

- Report and draft Bill published on 27 July 2010.[50]
- Holding response from Government 13 March 2015.[51]

48 (2016) LC 374.

49 (2014) LC 348.

50 (2010) LC 324.

51 Report on the Implementation of Law Commission Proposals, Ministry of Justice (2015), paragraph 99.

This project made recommendations for rationalising and simplifying the ways that judicial review and appeals by way of case stated can be used to challenge Crown Court decisions.

The Government is continuing to consider these recommendations.

Kidnapping

- Final report published 20 November 2014.[52]
- Awaiting a Government response.

The aim of the recommendations we made in our November 2014 report was to modernise the law on kidnapping and false imprisonment and address the gaps in the law relating to child abduction. Specifically, we recommended that:

- The kidnapping offence be redefined in statute but should remain triable in the Crown Court only.
- The existing offence of false imprisonment be replaced by a new statutory offence of unlawful detention.
- The maximum sentence for offences under sections 1 and 2 of the Child Abduction Act 1984 be increased from seven to 14 years' imprisonment.
- Section 1 of the 1984 Act be extended to cover cases involving the wrongful retention of a child abroad – this would close the gap in the law highlighted in the case of R (Nicolaou) v Redbridge Magistrates' Court.[53]

This work forms part of a wider project, Simplification of the Criminal Law, which originated in our 10th Programme of Law Reform. The Government has been considering the feasibility of our recommendations and aims to issue an interim response to the report in the near future.

Mental capacity and deprivation of liberty

- Final report published 13 March 2017.[54]
- Interim response from Government on 30 October 2017.

On 13 March 2017, we published our final report and draft Bill recommending that the DoLS be repealed with pressing urgency. The report sets out a replacement scheme for the DoLS – which we have called the Liberty Protection Safeguards. For more information see page 31.

The Government provided an interim response on 30 October 2017 acknowledging our work and noting that a final response should be expected in Spring 2018.

Offences against the person

- Scoping report and draft Bill published 3 November 2015.[55]
- Awaiting Government response.

This was a project for the modernisation and restatement of the main offences of violence, which are:

- Those contained in the Offences Against the Person Act 1861.
- The offences of assault and battery, which are common law offences.
- Assault on a constable, which is an offence under the Police Act 1996, section 89.

Our aim was to replace all these offences with a single modern and easily understandable statutory code largely based on a draft Bill published by the Home Office in 1998 but with some significant changes and updating.

We published our report in November 2015 and are awaiting a response from the Government.

52 Kidnapping and related Offences (2014) LC 355.

53 [2012] EWHC 1647 (Admin); [2012] 2 Cr App R 23.

54 (2017) LC 372.

55 (2015) LC 361.

Pension funds and social investment

- Final report published 21 June 2016.[56]

Our report found that barriers to social investment by pension funds are, in most cases, structural and behavioural rather than legal or regulatory. We identified steps which could be taken by Government, regulators and others to minimise these barriers. For more information on this project see page 16.

We currently await the Government's interim response, due December 2017.

Public nuisance and outraging public decency

- Final report published 24 June 2015.[57]
- Awaiting a Government response.

This report recommends retaining the offences and restating them in statute largely in their existing form. However, as the offences are serious ones, punishable by up to life imprisonment, the recommendations provide that the defendant should be liable only if there is proof of intention or recklessness. At present public nuisance only requires proof of negligence, and outraging public decency has no requirement of fault.

This work forms part of a wider project, Simplification of the Criminal Law, which originated in our 10th Programme of Law Reform. The Government is considering this report and will respond in due course.

Rights to light

- Final report and draft Bill published 4 December 2014.[58]
- Awaiting Government response.

Rights to light are easements that entitle landowners to receive natural light through defined apertures (most commonly windows) in buildings on their land. The owners of neighbouring properties cannot substantially interfere with the right, for example by erecting a building that blocks the light, without the consent of the landowner.

We commenced our project on rights to light in spring 2012.

We published our final report and draft Bill on 4 December 2014.[59]

We recommend:

- Establishing a statutory notice procedure allowing landowners to require their neighbours to tell them within a set time limit if they plan to seek an injunction to protect their right to light.
- Introducing a statutory test to clarify when the courts may order damages to be paid, rather than halting development or ordering a building to be demolished by granting an injunction (this takes into account the Supreme Court decision in the case of Coventry v Lawrence).[60]
- Updating the procedure whereby landowners can prevent their neighbours from acquiring rights to light by prescription.
- Amending the law governing when an unused right to light is to be treated as having been abandoned.
- Giving power to the Lands Chamber of the Upper Tribunal to discharge or modify obsolete or unused rights to light.

The Government has been carefully considering the report. There are no immediate plans to implement the recommendations as a result of other legislative priorities, but the position will be kept under review and discussions with the Commission are ongoing.

56 (2016) LC 374.

57 (2015) LC 358.

58 (2014) LC 356.

59 (2014) LC 356.

60 [2014] UKSC 13, [2014] 2 WLR 433.

Technical issues in charity law

- Final report published 14 September 2017.[61]
- Awaiting Government response.

Our report published in September 2017 seeks to address issues with the law within which charities operate. For more information on this project see page 27.

Termination of tenancies for tenant default

- Final report published 31 October 2006.[62]
- Awaiting Government response.

This project examined the means whereby a landlord can terminate a tenancy because the tenant has not complied with his or her obligations. This is an issue of great practical importance for many landlords and tenants of residential and commercial properties. The current law is difficult to use and littered with pitfalls for both the layperson and the unwary practitioner. It does not support negotiated settlement and provides insufficient protection for mortgagees and sub-tenants.

Our report recommended the abolition of forfeiture and its replacement by a modern statutory scheme for the termination of tenancies on the ground of tenant default that would balance the interests of all parties affected and promote more proportionate outcomes.

The Government's 2015 report on the implementation of our proposals identified some stakeholder concerns about the summary termination procedure proposed. The Government said in its report that it was considering how these concerns might be overcome.[63] Consideration of these issues is continuing and we await Government's decision.

Unfitness to plead

- Final report and draft Bill published 13 January 2016.[64]
- Interim Government response received on 22 February 2016.

The law relating to unfitness to plead addresses what should happen when a defendant who faces criminal prosecution is unable to engage with the process because of his or her mental or physical condition. The law aims to balance the rights of the vulnerable defendant with the interests of those affected by an alleged offence and the need to protect the public. However, the current law in this area is outdated, inconsistently applied and can lead to unfairness.

After a wide-ranging consultation conducted in winter 2010-11[65] we published an analysis of responses[66] and an issues paper in 2013[67] and our final report and draft Bill in January 2016.[68]

The Government provided an interim response on 22 February 2016, acknowledging our work and noting that a substantive response would be provided in due course.

61 (2017) LC 375.

62 (2006) LC 303.

63 Report on the implementation of Law Commission proposals, Ministry of Justice (2015) HC 1062.

64 (2016) LC 364 (two volumes).

65 (2010) LCCP 197.

66 http://www.lawcom.gov.uk/project/unfitness-to-plead/.

67 http://www.lawcom.gov.uk/project/unfitness-to-plead/.

68 (2016) LC 364 (two volumes).

OTHER REPORTS AND SCOPING PAPERS

Marriage law

- Scoping paper published 17 December 2015.
- Response from Government received on 11 September 2017.

This project involved a review of the law governing how and where people can marry in England and Wales.

We agreed to carry out an initial piece of work to prepare the way for potential future reform of this important area of law. Our preliminary study involved research into domestic and comparative law, and engagement with key stakeholders. The aim was to identify and analyse the issues that would need to be addressed in order to develop reform proposals as part of any future work. The work did not cover who can be married (for example, the age of consent to marry), the rights or responsibilities imparted by marriage (for example, the financial consequences of divorce), or whether religious groups should be obliged to solemnise marriages of same-sex couples.

We completed the initial phase of our work and published Getting Married: A Scoping Report at the end of 2015. We concluded that the law is in need of reform and we set out the issues that we would address in a future law reform project. The report comprises a list of questions to be addressed against the guiding principles of certainty and simplicity, fairness and equality, protecting the state's interest, and respecting individual wishes and beliefs.

A full project on reforming marriage law, under the new title of "Weddings" was put forward by us as a potential candidate for inclusion in our 13th Programme of Law Reform. However, on 11 September 2017, the Minister of State for Justice wrote to us to inform us that the MoJ does not currently support a full review. The Minister indicated that priority was being given to reforms to address the increase in public and private family law cases currently putting pressure on the justice system. We welcome the Minister's assurance that he will keep the possibility of further Law Commission work under review.

PART FOUR
How we work

The work of the Commission is grounded in thorough research and analysis of case law, legislation, academic and other writing, and other relevant sources of information both in the UK and overseas. It takes full account of the European Convention on Human Rights and relevant European law. Throughout this process, where appropriate, we act in consultation or work jointly with the Northern Ireland Law Commission and the Scottish Law Commission.

OUR PROGRAMME OF LAW REFORM

We are required to submit to the Lord Chancellor programmes for the examination of different branches of the law with a view to reform.

Every three or four years we consult widely, asking for suggestions for appropriate projects. During 2016-17 we have continued work on projects selected for our 12th Programme of Law Reform, which we launched in July 2014, and earlier programmes. Details of this work are set out in Part Two of this report. The full list of nine projects selected for our 12th Programme can be found in our annual report for 2014-15.[69] We opened the consultation for our 13th Programme on 14 July 2016.

Decisions about whether to include a particular subject in a programme of reform are based on:

- The strength of the need for law reform.
- The importance of the issues it will cover.
- The availability of resources in terms of both expertise and funding.
- Whether the project is suitable to be dealt with by the Commission.

Although we have a duty to "take and keep under review all the law",[70] it is important that our efforts are directed towards areas of the law that most need reform and reforms that are most likely to be implemented. We focus on change that will deliver real benefits to the people, businesses, organisations and institutions to which that law applies.

13th Programme

The consultation for this Programme of Law Reform received our largest ever response rate, with over 1,300 responses covering 220 individual suggestions for law reform projects. We have spent some time refining these suggestions, interacting closely with Government and stakeholders to test the need for law reform. We have also been working through options for collaborating with the Law Commission in Scotland, with whom we have developed strong links.

We had planned to seek the Lord Chancellor's approval for the 13th Programme during June and July. However, the general election meant that was not possible. We continued to refine the suggestions received as part of the consultation, interacting closely with Government and stakeholders to test the need for law reform.

We hope to be in a position to announce the 13th Programme before the end of the calendar year.

Consultation

We are committed to consulting fully with all the people and organisations potentially affected by our proposals. We engage with stakeholders from the outset of a project, even before a piece of work is officially adopted, and conduct thorough, targeted consultations throughout. This allows us to acquire a good understanding of the issues that are arising in an area of law and the effect they are having, and give us a clear picture of the context within which the law operates. We use them to assess the impact of our proposed policies and refine our thinking.

Our consultations can include meetings with individuals and organisations, public events, conferences, symposia and other types of event, as well as interviews and site visits. We often work through representative organisations, asking them to help us reach their members and stakeholders.

69 Annual Report 2014–15 (2015) LC 359, pp12-13.

70 Law Commissions Act 1965, s 3(1).

During our formal consultations we ask for written responses and provide a number of ways for consultees to submit these. All the responses we receive are analysed and considered carefully. Aggregated analyses are published on our website, and in some cases individual responses, usually alongside our final report.

We follow the Government Consultation Principles issued by the Cabinet Office.[71]

Making recommendations for reform

We set out our final recommendations in a report. If implementation of those recommendations would involve primary legislation, the report will usually contain a Bill drafted by our in-house Parliamentary Counsel. The report is laid before Parliament. It is then for Government to decide whether it accepts the recommendations and to introduce any necessary Bill in Parliament, unless an MP or Peer opts to do so.

After publication of a report the Commissioner, members of the relevant legal team and the Parliamentary Counsel who worked on the draft Bill will often give assistance to Government ministers and departments to help them take the work forward.

Other law reform projects

In addition to the law reform projects that make up our programme, we also undertake law reform projects that have been referred to us directly by Government departments.

During 2016-17, four projects were referred to us by Government:

- Pension Funds and Social Investment – an examination of whether there are any legal or regulatory barriers to pension schemes making social investments. This project was referred to us by the Department for Digital, Culture, Media and Sport (see page 16).
- Criminal Records Disclosure – a review of the filtering functions used as part of the criminal records disclosure system. This project was referred to us by the Home Office (see page 21).
- Search Warrants – a review to identify and address pressing problems with the law governing search warrants and to produce reform which will clarify and rationalise the law. This project was referred to us by the Home Office (see page 20).
- Protection of Official Data – a review of the law around the protection of official data, including the Official Secrets Act to ensure that the relevant statutes keep pace with the challenges of the 21st century. This project was referred to us by the Cabinet Office (see page 21).

71 https://www.gov.uk/government/publications/consultation-principles-guidance (last visited 7 April 2016).

Figure 4.1 Common stages of a law reform project

Initial informal consultation, approaching interest groups and specialists.

Project planning document agreed by the Law Commissioners.

Scoping work, defining the project's terms.

Formal consultation, making provisional proposals for reform.

Analyse responses to consultation.

Agree policy paper, setting out final recommendations for reform.

Instruct Parliamentary Counsel to produce draft Bill, if required.

Publish final report, making recommendations for reform, with:

- **An assessment of the impact of reform.**
- **An analysis of consultation responses.**
- **Usually, a draft Bill.**

Statute law

The Law Commission's statutory functions set out in section 3(1) of the Law Commissions Act 1965 include a duty "to prepare from time to time at the request of the Minister comprehensive programmes of consolidation and statute law revision, and to undertake the preparation of draft Bills pursuant to any such programme approved by the Minister".

Since its creation, the Law Commission has performed this important function of removing legislation that is obsolete or which has lost any modern purpose. The legislation appears to be still in force but this is misleading because it no longer has a job to do. This may be because the political, social or economic issue an Act was intended to address no longer exists or because an Act was intended to do a specific thing which, once done, means it has served its purpose.

Over time a vast body of legislation has built up; this is commonly referred to as the "statute book". Legislation that has no further function has not always been effectively cleared away. This can make things more costly, in terms of time and money, for those who work with the law. Also, an Act that still appears to have legal significance may entice people to rely on it, for example, as is becoming more common, where a person without the aid of a lawyer brings or defends a court case on the basis of a statutory right they think they have.

The work of the Law Commission improves the accuracy of the statute book so it can be used with greater confidence. As social and technological change continues to be reflected in new legislation, and as internet access to statutory law increases its availability, the need for systematic and expert review of existing legislation will continue.

Statute law repeals

This work is carried out by a dedicated team. Candidates for repeal are identified and researched. The legal background to an Act is examined, as well as the historical and social circumstances which might have led to it. We consult on proposed repeals and then prepare a draft Bill. The repeals are carried out by means of Statute Law (Repeals) Bills. Nineteen of these Acts have been enacted so far, between them repealing over 3,000 Acts in their entirety and partially repealing thousands of others.

In future, our statute law repeals work is likely to narrow its focus. Work will be concentrated on the repeal of Acts and provisions where it is most needed and where it brings the greatest benefit. Priority candidates for repeal will be dead law that creates a risk of misleading the broadest range of those who rely on the statute book, whether that is in a professional or private capacity.

Consolidation

Between its establishment in 1965 and 2006, we have been responsible for 220 consolidation Acts. Since then only two have been produced: the Charities Act 2011 and the Co-operative and Community Benefit Societies Act 2014. This change reflects the fact that, in a time of reduced funding in most areas of public services and, specifically, reduced core funding for the Law Commission, consolidation on the old-fashioned model can no longer be considered a priority.

However, the need for simplification of the law is as great as it ever has been. The pattern in future is likely to be codification rather than a simple consolidation in areas where statute law is incoherent or confusing and where codification would bring genuine practical benefits.

Implementation

Crucial to the implementation of our consolidation and statue law repeals Bills is a dedicated parliamentary procedure. The Bill is introduced into the House of Lords and, after Lords Second Reading, is scrutinised by the Joint Committee on Consolidation Bills. The Committee is appointed by both Houses specifically to consider consolidation and statute law repeal Bills and will hear evidence from the Law Commission. After this, the Bill returns to the House of Lords and continues through the remaining stages.

THE LAW COMMISSION AND GOVERNMENT

Government response to Law Commission reports

In March 2010 we agreed a statutory Protocol[72] with the Lord Chancellor that governs how the Commission and Government Departments should work together on law reform projects. The latter part of the Protocol sets out departmental responsibilities once we have published a report. The minister for the relevant department will provide an interim response to us as soon as possible but not later than six months after publication of the report. We expect to receive a final response within a year of the report being published.

Improving the prospects of implementation

The Protocol also requires that, where we are considering taking on a law reform project, the relevant department will give an undertaking that there is a "serious intention" to take forward reform in that area of law. While this is not a guarantee that the Government will accept or implement our recommendations for reform, it enables us to commit resources to a project in the knowledge that we have a reasonable expectation of implementation.

Accounting to Parliament for implementation

The Law Commission Act 2009 requires the Lord Chancellor to report annually to Parliament on the extent to which our proposals have been implemented by the Government. The report must set out the Government's reasons for decisions taken during the year to accept or reject our proposals and give an indication of when decisions can be expected on recommendations that are still being considered. The Lord Chancellor issued the sixth of these reports on 12 January 2017.[73]

72 Protocol between the Lord Chancellor (on behalf of the Government) and the Law Commission (2010) LC 321.

73 https://www.gov.uk/government/collections/implementation-of-the-law-commission-proposals (last visited 13 April 2016).

The Law Commission and the Welsh Government

The Wales Act 2014 provides for a protocol[74] to be established between the Law Commission and the Welsh Government. This protocol was agreed and presented to the National Assembly for Wales on 10 July 2015. It sets out the approach that we and Welsh ministers jointly take to our law reform work. It covers how the relationship works throughout all the stages of a project, from our decision to take on a piece of work, through to the ministers' response to our final report and recommendations.

In a direct reflection of the obligations placed on the Lord Chancellor by the Law Commission Act 2009, the 2014 Act also requires Welsh ministers to report annually to the Assembly about the implementation of our reports relating to Welsh devolved matters. The second Welsh Government Report on the Implementation of Law Commission Proposals/ Adroddiad ar weithredu cynigion Comisiwn y Gyfraith was laid before the Assembly on 16 February 2017.

INFORMING DEBATE AND SCRUTINY

We are often invited to give evidence to special committees to assist with their inquiries and their consideration of Bills, some of which may include provisions that have derived from Law Commission recommendations.

THE LAW COMMISSIONERS

The five Law Commissioners work full time at the Law Commission, except that the Chair sits as a judge for one working week in four.

In accordance with Government policy for all non-departmental public bodies, there is a Code of Best Practice for Law Commissioners. It incorporates the Seven Principles of Public Life and covers matters such as the role and responsibilities of Commissioners.[75]

EXTERNAL RELATIONS

We work hard to establish strong links with a wide range of organisations and individuals who have an interest in law reform, and greatly value these relationships. We are indebted to all those who send us feedback on our consultation papers, contribute project ideas for our programmes of law reform, and provide input and expertise at all stages of the process of making recommendations to Government.

It would not be possible in this annual report to thank individually everyone who provides us with guidance or offers us their views. We would, however, like to express our gratitude to our Welsh Advisory Committee and all those organisations and individuals who have worked with us as members of advisory groups on our many projects and who have contributed in so many ways to our work during the course of the year.

We also acknowledge the support and interest shown in the Commission and our work by a number of Ministers at Westminster and in Cardiff, Members of Parliament and of the Welsh Assembly and Peers from across the political spectrum, and by public officials. We continue to make progress in extending the number of ways in which we engage with our friends and supporters.

COMMUNICATIONS

Since 1965 we have changed the lives of many people by reforming the law for the better. Underpinning this is the need to communicate effectively to enable greater public engagement in our consultations, create awareness of what we do amongst Government departments and build momentum behind our recommendations for reform.

As a result a new two-year communications strategy was approved in 2017. This set out how to restructure the communications offering based on the industry best practice – the Government Communications Service MCOM.

74 Protocol rhwng Gweinidogion Cymru a Comisiwn y Gyfraith/Protocol between the Welsh Ministers and the Law Commission (2015).

75 http://www.lawcom.gov.uk/about/who-we-are.

Already it is paying dividends across our campaigning and marketing channels. Sessions on our website are up 15% in 2017. We have 6,000 new subscribers to receive automatic updates about our work –16,024 in total. Our Twitter account has now also reached 12,800 followers, up from 9,500 last year. This is alongside two positive front pages in national media and hundreds of items across broadcast, national, local and trade media informing people of our work.

SCARMAN LECTURE

The sixth Scarman Lecture was held on 26 June 2017 at Gray's Inn. In honour of the Law Commission's founder, every two years or so the Commission invites one of the world's most distinguished lawyers to deliver a talk to senior members of the judiciary, Parliamentarians, civil servants and others within the legal profession.

This year we had the privilege of hearing the Lord Chief Justice of England and Wales, Lord Thomas of Cwmgiedd discuss a vision for law reform in the post-Brexit world and the importance of maintaining the pre-eminence of English law in the digital era. For more information on the Scarman Lecture, see page 58.

ALUMNI

We are keen to hear from our former colleagues. We would like to encourage all former Law Commission colleagues to keep in touch with us through our alumni group on LinkedIn.

EDUCATION AND ENGAGMENT

We have a statutory duty to promote the reform of the law and continue to work hard in this area. Alongside the production of various infographics to explain in plain English each new law reform project, we speak to students and practitioners from across Britain and the world.

Over the past year or so this has involved:

- Helping to set the standards for law reform globally by contributing extensively to the Commonwealth Law Reform Guide.
- Once again supporting the Big Voice Model Law Commission project. A volunteer-led project to spark sixth formers' interest in issues of legal identity and the process of law reform.
- Speaking at sessions at universities across the country as well as hosting a group of international undergraduate students from Rice University, Texas.
- Hosting sessions for international law reformers from China, South America and across the world.
- Training at the Judicial College to emphasise the importance of law reform to some of the country's leading legal experts.

SPEAKING ON LAW REFORM

As an outward-facing organisation the Commission's Chair, Commissioners and staff have been active speaking at many different events across the country.

Over 2016-17, highlights include:

- The annual Legal Wales conference in both 2016 and 2017.
- A series of public and practitioner consultation events for the launch of our Wills project.
- A series of consultations reaching over a thousand practitioners in England and Wales for the Sentencing Code project.
- A keynote speech at the Retirement Housing Group conference about our Event Fees in Retirement Properties report.

- Setting out how the Commission works at the Bar Council's annual conference 2017.

SOCIAL RESPONSIBILITY

Every year a team, made up of our legal and other staff, joins members of the judiciary and teams from many of London's law firms and sets of chambers in the annual London Legal Walk. In 2016 the team raised more than £1,000 for the London Legal Support Trust, which organises the event. The funds go to support free legal advice agencies in and around London, including Law Centres and pro bono advice surgeries.

Our staff have also come together to raise funds for other causes during the year, in a variety of ways, for example a very successful baking day in aid of Macmillan.

OUR PARTNER LAW COMMISSIONS AND THE DEVOLVED AUTHORITIES

In June 2016 the Chair and Chief Executive attended the Five Jurisdictions Conference of Law Commissions in Jersey alongside colleagues from the other four law reform bodies of Jersey, Northern Ireland, the Republic of Ireland and Scotland. This is an annual event that allows us to exchange experiences and strengthen our relationships.

We continue to work closely with our colleagues in the Scottish Law Commission, seeking views as appropriate and engaging on a regular basis.

The Scarman Lecture

On 26 June the Law Commission welcomed distinguished guests to the sixth Scarman Lecture, "'Law Reform Now' in 21st century Britain: Brexit and Beyond", given by the Lord Chief Justice of England and Wales, the Lord Thomas of Cwmgiedd.

Every two years or so the Commission hosts a lecture by one of the world's leading law reformers, in honour of Lord Scarman, the first Chair.

Founded in in 2006, the first four lectures were given by judges of exceptional distinction from other jurisdictions: Justices Aharon Barak, Edwin Cameron, Ruth Bader Ginsburg and Michael Kirby. The fifth was given by Sir Geoffrey Palmer, a former Prime Minister of New Zealand who became Chair of the New Zealand Law Commission.

But this year we looked closer to home for a great law reformer.

To a packed hall of more than 120 members of the senior judiciary, lawyers, Parliamentarians and Government officials, Lord Thomas shed light on some of the pressing legal issues of the day.

In one of his last speeches before retirement, the Lord Chief Justice focused on two main themes:

- A vision for law reform in the post-Brexit Government.
- The importance of maintaining the pre-eminence of English Law in the digital era.

In a lecture lasting a little over an hour, the most senior member of the judiciary spoke with passion about the future. He described Brexit as "without doubt" the most complex peacetime issue the UK has ever faced in legal terms. He put commerce at the forefront and stressed that the UK must ensure its laws remain the "law of choice 'for modern ways'" and "a law of choice for international commerce".

As we leave the European Union, and as the digital revolution gathers pace, the Lord Chief Justice said that the law must keep pace with rest of the world. Our laws must retain at least "an equivalence, if not better" with other jurisdictions.

Acknowledging that this was no small task, Lord Thomas called for a non-Government body to oversee the task. He said that politicians should consider a long-term role for the Law Commission as the body charged with ensuring that our laws meet such "radical and fundamental changes".[76]

76 The full text of the Scarman lecture can be found here: https://www.lawcom.gov.uk/lectures-talks/law-reform-now-in-21st-century-britain-brexit-and-beyond/

Who was Lord Scarman?

Leslie Scarman was born in July 1911 in Streatham. After graduating with a double first class degree from Brasenose College, Oxford, he was called to the Bar by Middle Temple in 1936. He joined up at the outbreak of the Second World War and in 1945, as an RAF staff officer, was present at the signing of the German surrender. He returned to civilian life in what is now Fountain Court Chambers and built up a practice ranging from planning to aviation law. In 1961 he was appointed a judge of the Probate, Divorce and Admiralty Division. He was appointed as the first Chair of the Law Commission from 1965 to 1973 and set the law reform model throughout the Commonwealth. He was promoted to the Court of Appeal in 1973 and the House of Lords in 1977. He led four major public inquiries over his life, the most famous of which concerned the Brixton Riots of April 1981. The report which he produced only seven months later was described by a national newspaper as “one of the great social documents of our time”.

> Since its creation, the Law Commission has made a signal contribution to the reform and development of our law. As a consequence it is in much better shape than it was in 1963.

Lord Chief Justice of England and Wales
Rt Hon Lord Thomas of Cwmgied
Scarman Lecture, June 2017.

Part Five
Our people and corporate matters

The Law Commission is grateful to everyone within the organisation for their hard work, expertise and support as well as their contribution to the work of the Commission.

BUDGET

The Law Commission's core funding, provided to us by Parliament and received through the MoJ, for 2016-17 was £2.67 million. The cost of the Commission can be found at Appendix B.

Alongside the rest of Government, we felt the initial impact of the Spending Review 2015. In 2016-17 our budget fell by 8% as compared to 2015-16. In order to protect our law reform capability, it was necessary to look at non-legal resources as a means of meeting our spending review obligations. This led to the restructuring of the corporate services team, as outlined later in this part of the report.

STAFF AT THE COMMISSION

The Commissioners are supported by the staff of the Law Commission. The staff are civil servants and are led by a Chief Executive.

In 2016-17 there were 51 people working at the Law Commission (full-time equivalent: 49.0 as at 31 March 2017).[77]

Figure 5.1 People working at the Commission (full-time equivalent, at 31 March 2017)

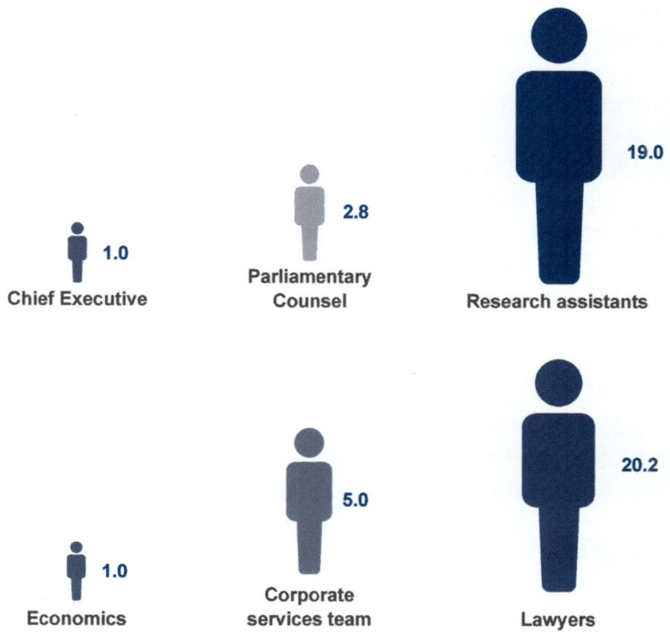

Figure 5.2 Lawyers (full-time equivalent, at 1 April 2016)

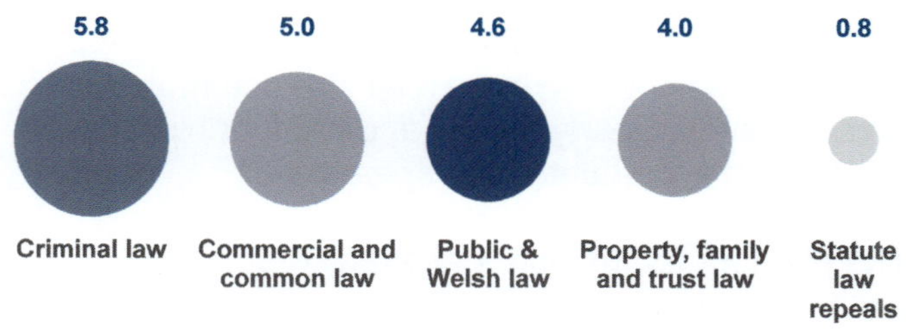

77 Excluding the Chair, Chair's Clerk and Commissioners.

Chief Executive

Our Chief Executive is responsible for setting the strategic direction of the Commission, in discussion with the Chair and other Commissioners, and for staffing, funding, organisation and management. The Chief Executive is the Commission's Budget Holder. He is also responsible for the day-to-day management of the Law Commission's relationship with the MoJ, including liaising with and influencing senior Departmental officials and promoting contacts and influence within Government departments.

Our Chief Executive provides advice and assistance to the Chair and other Commissioners, including support of the Chair in his relationships with ministers, the senior judiciary, relevant Parliamentary committees and the media.

Legal staff

Our lawyers are barristers, solicitors or legal academics from a wide range of professional backgrounds, including private practice and public service.

We organise the legal staff into five teams to support the Commissioners: commercial and common law; criminal law; property, family and trust; public and Welsh law; and statute law repeals.

The first four teams undertake law reform work, each with one Commissioner responsible for the work of the team. Each of these four teams is led by a team manager, a senior lawyer who provides direct support to the relevant Commissioner and leads the team of lawyers and research assistants working with the Commissioner to deliver their projects. Team managers generally do not lead on specific law reform projects themselves; their role focuses on project managing the team's work, providing legal and policy input into those projects, recruiting, mentoring and managing staff and working with the Chief Executive on corporate matters. The team managers also lead on relationships with key stakeholders inside and outside Government for the projects in their area. Team managers report to the Chief Executive.

Individual lawyers within teams, and occasionally Commissioners, lead on law reform projects. They will, with the support of a research assistant, research the law, lead on the development and drafting of policy proposals and papers, and liaise with key stakeholders alongside the team manager. The lawyers will undertake much of the day-to-day work on a law reform project.

The statute law repeals team is also headed by a team manager lawyer. Historically, the Chair has taken overall responsibility for the work of that team.

We are fortunate to have in-house Parliamentary Counsel who prepare the draft Bills attached to the law reform reports, and who are seconded to the Law Commission from the Office of the Parliamentary Counsel. We are delighted to have their expertise available to us.

Research assistants

Each year a number of well-qualified graduates are recruited to assist with research, drafting and creative thinking. They generally spend a year or two at the Commission before moving on to further their legal training and careers.

For many research assistants, working at the Commission has been a significant rung on the ladder to a highly successful career.

The selection process is extremely thorough and we aim to attract a diverse range of candidates of the highest calibre through contact with faculty careers advisers, as well as through our website and social media channels, and by placing articles in the relevant media. A comprehensive outreach programme was undertaken as part of the 2017 recruitment process, targeting law faculties at a wider range of universities as well as an improved and more modern social media campaign.

In 2016-17 we recruited 14 research assistants and the 2017-18 intake of 14 research assistants have recently joined the Commission.

We recognise the contribution our research assistants make, particularly through their enthusiastic commitment to the work of law reform and their lively participation in debate.

Economic and analytical services

The Commission benefits from the expertise of an economist who provides specialist advice in relation to the assessment of the impact of our proposals for law reform. As a member of the Government Economic Service, our economist also provides an essential link with the MoJ and other Government department analytical teams.

Corporate services

2016-17 was a year of change for the corporate services team, which for these purposes also includes the Head of Communications, Head of Strategic Engagement and Head of Strategic Planning roles. During 2016, a restructure of the team took place that led to considerable change for almost all of the roles in the team, as well as a 50% reduction in size.

Despite these reductions, the team is still able to provide effective corporate support in relation to the following activities:

- Governance.
- Transformation.
- Strategy.
- Human Resources.
- Information Technology.
- Financial Management.
- Internal, external and strategic communications.
- Knowledge and records management.
- Information assurance.
- Health and safety.
- Business continuity.

SENIOR MANAGEMENT TEAM

Our senior management team is formed of the Chief Executive, legal team managers, the corporate services team manager, Parliamentary Counsel and the economist. The team meets twice a month and take decisions on the day-to-day running of the Commission as well as reviewing all programme and project planning relating to our law reform projects.

WORKING AT THE COMMISSION

Staff engagement

The results of the annual People Survey show the Law Commission with an engagement index of 69% for 2016. This represented a 6% fall from the previous year, almost certainly due to wide scale structural changes that happened during 2016. It still places us as a high-performing organisation compared to other organisations of a similar size within the Civil Service. However more detailed work was clearly needed to better understand the issues impacting on staff.

Following the People Survey, a number of focus groups were held with people from across the Commission to help shape our people action plan for the year. A number of ideas were put forward to address our target areas – Learning and Development; Inclusion and Fair Treatment, Leadership and Managing Change and Internal Communications. A People Survey Action Group has been created to monitor and report on progress in implementing the actions.

In addition, to help our staff maintain a good work-life balance, we also offer a wide variety of flexible working arrangements such as home-working, part-time and compressed hours.

Investing in our people

The Law Commission is keen to invest in the continuing professional development of all our staff. In addition to providing access to formal training, we run a series of lunchtime seminars throughout the year and have been building on our efforts during 2017.

We invite contributors from the legal, parliamentary and academic worlds, as well as asking our colleagues within the Commission to share their considerable expertise.

WHISTLEBLOWING

All civil servants are bound by the Civil Service Code, which sets out the core values – integrity, honesty, objectivity and impartiality – expected of all MoJ employees.

Staff are encouraged to raise immediately any concerns they have about wrongdoing or breaches of the Civil Service Code by following the whistleblowing procedure. We follow the MoJ whistleblowing procedure, which is made available to all staff via the Law Commission intranet.

FREEDOM OF INFORMATION

The Freedom of Information Act encourages public authorities to make as much information as possible available to the public. Under the Act, we are required to adopt a publication scheme that contains information we routinely make available, and ensure that information is published in accordance with the scheme.

We make a significant amount of information available under our publication scheme. One of its benefits is that it makes information easily accessible and free-of-charge to the public, which removes the need for a formal Freedom of Information request to be made.

The Information Commissioner's Office has developed and approved a model publication scheme that all public authorities must adopt. We have adopted this scheme and we use the definition document for non-departmental public bodies to identify the type of information that we should publish. Among this is a quarterly disclosure log of requests made under the Freedom of Information Act that we have received and dealt with. More details can be found on our website.

INFORMATION ASSURANCE

In 2016-17 we reported a total of four notifiable incidents, all of which related to the loss of building passes. None of these incidents involved any loss of data.

HEALTH AND SAFETY

During the year, there were no notifiable incidents in relation to staff of the Commission and the Health and Safety at Work etc Act 1974.

SUSTAINABILITY

Our actions in relation to energy saving contribute to the overall reduction in consumption across the MoJ estate.

Paper is widely recycled in the office. All our publications are printed on paper containing a minimum of 75% recycled fibre content, and we are actively exploring ways to reduce the quantity of our printed materials.

Sir David Bean, Chair

Professor
David Ormerod QC

Professor Nick Hopkins

Nicholas Paines QC

Stephen Lewis

Phillip Golding
Chief Executive

APPENDICES

Appendix A

Implementation status of Law Commission law reform reports

LC No	Title	Status	Related measures
	2017		
375	Technical issues in Charity Law	Pending	
374	Pension Funds and Social Investment	Pending	
373	Event Fees in Retirement Properties	Pending	
372	Mental Capacity and Deprivation of Liberty	Pending	
371	Criminal Records Disclosures: Non-Filterable Offences	Pending	
	2016		
370	Enforcement of Family Financial Orders	Pending	
369	Bills of Sale	Accepted	
368	Consumer Prepayments on Retailer Insolvency	Pending	
366	Form and Accessibility of the Law Applicable in Wales	Accepted	
365	A New Sentencing Code for England and Wales Transition	Superseded	
364	Unfitness to Plead	Pending	
	2015		
363	Firearms Law – Reforms to Address Pressing Problems	Implemented	Policing and Crime Act 2017 (Part 6)
362	Wildlife Law	Implemented in part, rejected in part	Infrastructure Act 2015
361	Reform of Offences against the Person (HC 555)	Pending	
360	Patents, Trade Marks and Designs: Unjustified Threats	Implemented	Intellectual Property (Unjustified Threats) Act 2017
358	Simplification of Criminal Law: Public Nuisance and Outraging Public Decency	Pending	
	2014		
356	Rights to Light (HC 796)	Pending	
355	Simplification of Criminal Law: Kidnapping and Related Offences	Pending	
No LC Number	Social Investment by Charities	Implemented	Charities (Protection and Social Investment) Act 2016
353	Insurance Contract Law (Cm 8898;SG/2014/131)	Implemented	Insurance Act 2015; Enterprise Act 2016
351	Data Sharing between Public Bodies: A Scoping Report	Pending	

LC No	Title	Status	Related measures
350	Fiduciary Duties of Investment Intermediaries (HC 368)	Accepted	
349	Conservation Covenants (HC 322)	Pending	
348	Hate Crime: Should the Current Offences be Extended? (Cm 8865)	Pending	
347	Taxi and Private Hire Services (Cm 8864)	Accepted in part; pending in part	Deregulation Act 2015
346	Patents, Trade Marks and Design Rights: Groundless Threats (Cm 8851)	Superseded	Superseded by LC360
345	Regulation of Health Care Professionals: Regulation of Social Care Professionals in England (Cm 8839 / SG/2014/26 / NILC 18 (2014))	Accepted	
344	Contempt of Court (2): Court Reporting (HC 1162)	Pending	
343	Matrimonial Property, Needs and Agreements (HC 1039)	Implemented in part; pending in part	
342	Wildlife Law: Control of Invasive Non-native Species (HC 1039)	Implemented	Infrastructure Act 2015
	2013		
340	Contempt of Court (1): Juror Misconduct and Internet Publications (HC 860)	Implemented	Criminal Justice and Courts Act 2015
339	Level Crossings (Cm 8711)	Pending	
337	Renting Homes in Wales/Rhentu Cartrefi yng Nghymru (Cm 8578)	Implemented	Renting Homes (Wales) Act 2016
336	The Electronic Communications Code (HC 1004)	Implemented	Digital Economy Act 2017
	2012		
335	Contempt of Court: Scandalising the Court (HC 839)	Implemented	Crime and Courts Act 2013 (s 33)
332	Consumer Redress for Misleading and Aggressive Practices (Cm 8323)	Implemented	Consumer Protection (Amendment) Regulations 2014; Consumer Rights Act 2015
	2011		
331	Intestacy and Family Provision Claims on Death (HC 1674)	Implemented in part	Inheritance and Trustees' Powers Act 2014
329	Public Service Ombudsmen (HC 1136)	Pending	
327	Making Land Work: Easements, Covenants and Profits à Prendre (HC 1067)	Accepted	
326	Adult Social Care (HC 941)	Implemented	Care Act 2014 and Social Services and Well-Being (Wales) Act 2014
325	Expert Evidence in Criminal Proceedings in England and Wales (HC 829)	Implemented	Criminal Procedure Rules
	2010		
324	The High Court's Jurisdiction in Relation to Criminal Proceedings (HC 329)	Pending	
322	Administrative Redress: Public Bodies and the Citizen (HC 6)	Rejected	
320	The Illegality Defence (HC 412)	Rejected	

LC No	Title	Status	Related measures
	2009		
319	Consumer Insurance Law: Pre-Contract Disclosure and Misrepresentation (Cm 7758)	Implemented	Consumer Insurance (Disclosure and Representation) Act 2012 (c6)
318	Conspiracy and Attempts (HC 41)	Accepted but will not be implemented	
317	Consumer Remedies for Faulty Goods (Cm 7725)	Implemented	Consumer Rights Act 2015
315	Capital and Income in Trusts: Classification and Apportionment (HC 426)	Implemented	Trusts (Capital and Income) Act 2013
314	Intoxication and Criminal Liability (Cm 7526)	Rejected	
	2008		
313	Reforming Bribery (HC 928)	Implemented	Bribery Act 2010 (c23)
312	Housing: Encouraging Responsible Letting (Cm 7456)	Rejected	
309	Housing: Proportionate Dispute Resolution (Cm 7377)	Accepted in part	
	2007		
307	Cohabitation: The Financial Consequences of Relationship Breakdown (Cm 7182)	Pending	
305	Participating in Crime (Cm 7084)	Pending	
	2006		
304	Murder, Manslaughter and Infanticide (HC 30)	Implemented in part	Coroners and Justice Act 2009 (c25)
303	Termination of Tenancies (Cm 6946)	Pending	
302	Post-Legislative Scrutiny (Cm 6945)	Implemented	See Post-Legislative Scrutiny: The Government's Approach (2008) Cm 7320
301	Trustee Exemption Clauses (Cm 6874)	Implemented	See Written Answer, Hansard (HC), 14 September 2010, vol 515, col 38WS
300	Inchoate Liability for Assisting and Encouraging Crime (Cm 6878)	Implemented	Serious Crime Act 2007 (c27)
297	Renting Homes: The Final Report (Cm 6781)	Rejected for England, Accepted in principle for Wales	
	2005		
296	Company Security Interests (Cm 6654)	Pending	
295	The Forfeiture Rule and the Law of Succession (Cm 6625)	Implemented	Estates of Deceased Persons (Forfeiture Rule and Law of Succession) Act 2011
292	Unfair Terms in Contracts (SLC 199) (Cm 6464; SE/2005/13)	Implemented	Consumer Rights Act 2015
	2004		
291	Towards a Compulsory Purchase Code: (2) Procedure (Cm 6406)	Accepted but will not be implemented	
290	Partial Defences to Murder (Cm 6301)	Implemented	Coroners and Justice Act 2009 (c25)

LC No	Title	Status	Related measures
	2006		
288	In the Public Interest: Publication of Local Authority Inquiry Reports (Cm 6274)	Accepted but will not be implemented	
	2004		
287	Pre-judgment Interest on Debts and Damages (HC 295)	Rejected	
	2003		
286	Towards a Compulsory Purchase Code: (1) Compensation (Cm 6071)	Accepted but will not be implemented	
284	Renting Homes (Cm 6018)	Superseded	See LC 297
283	Partnership Law (SLC192) (Cm 6015; SE/2003/299)	Implemented in part; Accepted in part; Rejected in part	The Legislative Reform (Limited Partnerships) Order 2009
282	Children: Their Non-accidental Death or Serious Injury (Criminal Trials) (HC 1054)	Implemented	Domestic Violence, Crime and Victims Act 2004 (c28)
281	Land, Valuation and Housing Tribunals: The Future (Cm 5948)	Rejected	
	2002		
277	The Effective Prosecution of Multiple Offending (Cm 5609)	Implemented	Domestic Violence, Crime and Victims Act 2004 (c28)
276	Fraud (Cm 5560)	Implemented in part	Fraud Act 2006 (c35)
	2001		
273	Evidence of Bad Character in Criminal Proceedings (Cm 5257)	Implemented	Criminal Justice Act 2003 (c44)
272	Third Parties – Rights against Insurers (SLC 184) (Cm 5217)	Implemented	Third Parties (Rights Against Insurers) Act 2010 (c10); Third Parties (Rights against Insurers) Regulations 2016
271	Land Registration for the Twenty-First Century (jointly with HM Land Registry) (HC 114)	Implemented	Land Registration Act 2002 (c9)
270	Limitation of Actions (HC 23)	Rejected	
269	Bail and the Human Rights Act 1998 (HC 7)	Implemented	Criminal Justice Act 2003 (c44)
267	Double Jeopardy and Prosecution Appeals (Cm 5048)	Implemented	Criminal Justice Act 2003 (c44)
	1999		
263	Claims for Wrongful Death (HC 807)	Rejected	
262	Damages for Personal Injury: Medical and Nursing Expenses (HC 806)	Rejected	
261	Company Directors: Regulating Conflicts of Interests (SLC 173) (Cm 4436; SE/1999/25)	Implemented	Companies Act 2006 (c46)
260	Trustees' Powers and Duties (SLC 172) (HC 538; SE2)	Implemented	Trustee Act 2000 (c29)
257	Damages for Personal Injury: Non-Pecuniary Loss (HC 344)	Implemented in part	See Heil v Rankin [2000] 3 WLR 117
	1998		
255	Consents to Prosecution (HC 1085)	Accepted (Advisory only, no draft Bill)	
253	Execution of Deeds and Documents (Cm 4026)	Implemented	Regulatory Reform (Execution of Deeds and Documents) Order 2005

LC No	Title	Status	Related measures
251	The Rules against Perpetuities and Excessive Accumulations (HC 579)	Implemented	Perpetuities and Accumulations Act 2009 (c18)
249	Liability for Psychiatric Illness (HC 525)	Rejected	
248	Corruption (HC 524)	Superseded	See LC 313
	1997		
247	Aggravated, Exemplary and Restitutionary Damages (HC 346)	Rejected	
246	Shareholder Remedies (Cm 3759)	Implemented	Companies Act 2006 (c46)
245	Evidence in Criminal Proceedings: Hearsay (Cm 3670)	Implemented	Criminal Justice Act 2003 (c44)
	1996		
243	Money Transfers (HC 690)	Implemented	Theft (Amendment) Act 1996 (c62)
242	Contracts for the Benefit of Third Parties (Cm 3329)	Implemented	Contracts (Rights of Third Parties) Act 1999 (c31)
238	Responsibility for State and Condition of Property (HC 236)	Accepted in part but will not be implemented; Rejected in part	
237	Involuntary Manslaughter (HC 171)	Implemented in part	Corporate Manslaughter and Corporate Homicide Act 2007 (c19); see LC 304
	1995		
236	Fiduciary Duties and Regulatory Rules (Cm 3049)	Rejected	
235	Land Registration: First Joint Report with HM Land Registry (Cm 2950)	Implemented	Land Registration Act 1997 (c2)
231	Mental Incapacity (HC 189)	Implemented	Mental Capacity Act 2005 (c9)
230	The Year and a Day Rule in Homicide (HC 183)	Implemented	Law Reform (Year and a Day Rule) Act 1996 (c19)
229	Intoxication and Criminal Liability (HC 153)	Superseded	See LC 314
	1994		
228	Conspiracy to Defraud (HC 11)	Implemented	Theft (Amendment) Act 1996 (c62)
227	Restitution: Mistakes of Law (Cm 2731)	Implemented in part	See Kleinwort Benson v Lincoln City Council [1999] 2 AC 349
226	Judicial Review (HC 669)	Implemented in part	Housing Act 1996 (c52); Access to Justice Act 1999 (c22); Tribunals, Courts and Enforcement Act 2007 (c15)
224	Structured Settlements (Cm 2646)	Implemented	Finance Act 1995 (c4); Civil Evidence Act 1995 (c38); Damages Act 1996 (c48)
222	Binding Over (Cm 2439)	Implemented in part	In March 2007, the President of the Queen's Bench Division issued a Practice Direction
221	Termination of Tenancies (HC 135)	Superseded	See LC 303
220	Delegation by Individual Trustees (HC 110)	Implemented	Trustee Delegation Act 1999 (c15)

LC No	Title	Status	Related measures
	1993		
219	Contributory Negligence as a Defence in Contract (HC 9)	Rejected	
218	Legislating the Criminal Code: Offences against the Person and General Principles (Cm 2370)	Implemented in part	Domestic Violence Crime and Victims Act 2004 (c28)
217	Effect of Divorce on Wills (Cm 2322)	Implemented	Law Reform (Succession) Act 1995 (c41)
216	The Hearsay Rule in Civil Proceedings (Cm 2321)	Implemented	Civil Evidence Act 1995 (c38)
215	Sale of Goods Forming Part of a Bulk (SLC 145) (HC 807)	Implemented	Sale of Goods (Amendment) Act 1995 (c28)
	1992		
208	Business Tenancies (HC 224)	Implemented	Regulatory Reform (Business Tenancies) (England and Wales) Order 2003
207	Domestic Violence and Occupation of the Family Home (HC 1)	Implemented	Family Law Act 1996 (c27), Part IV
205	Rape within Marriage (HC 167)	Implemented	Criminal Justice and Public Order Act 1994 (c33)
	1991		
204	Land Mortgages (HC 5)	Rejected	
202	Corroboration of Evidence in Criminal Trials (Cm 1620)	Implemented	Criminal Justice and Public Order Act 1994 (c33)
201	Obsolete Restrictive Covenants (HC 546)	Rejected	
199	Transfer of Land: Implied Covenants for Title (HC 437)	Implemented	Law of Property (Miscellaneous Provisions) Act 1994 (c36)
196	Rights of Suit: Carriage of Goods by Sea (SLC 130) (HC 250)	Implemented	Carriage of Goods by Sea Act 1992 (c50)
194	Distress for Rent (HC 138)	Implemented in part	Tribunals, Courts and Enforcement Act 2007 (c15), Part III (enacted, but not yet brought into force)
	1990		
193	Private International Law: Choice of Law in Tort and Delict (SLC 129) (HC 65)	Implemented	Private International Law (Miscellaneous Provisions) Act 1995 (c42)
192	Family Law: The Ground for Divorce (HC 636)	Implemented	Family Law Act 1996 (c27), Part II (enacted, but never brought into force)
	1989		
188	Overreaching: Beneficiaries in Occupation (HC 61)	Implemented in part	Trusts of Land and Appointment of Trustees Act 1996 (c47)
187	Distribution on Intestacy (HC 60)	Implemented in part	Law Reform (Succession) Act 1995 (c41)
186	Computer Misuse (Cm 819)	Implemented	Computer Misuse Act 1990 (c18)
184	Title on Death (Cm 777)	Implemented	Law of Property (Miscellaneous Provisions) Act 1994 (c36)

LC No	Title	Status	Related measures
181	Trusts of Land (HC 391)	Implemented	Trusts of Land and Appointment of Trustees Act 1996 (c47)
180	Jurisdiction over Offences of Fraud and Dishonesty with a Foreign Element (HC 318)	Implemented	Criminal Justice Act 1993 (c36), Part I
178	Compensation for Tenants' Improvements (HC 291)	Rejected	
177	Criminal Law: A Criminal Code (2 vols) (HC 299)	Superseded	Superseded by the criminal law simplification project: see Tenth Programme.
	1988		
175	Matrimonial Property (HC 9)	Rejected	
174	Landlord and Tenant: Privity of Contract and Estate (HC 8)	Implemented	Landlord and Tenant (Covenants) Act 1995 (c30)
173	Property Law: Fourth Report on Land Registration (HC 680)	Superseded	See LC 235
172	Review of Child Law: Guardianship (HC 594)	Implemented	Children Act 1989 (c41)
	1987		
168	Private International Law: Law of Domicile (SLC 107) (Cm 200)	Rejected	
166	Transfer of Land: The Rule in Bain v Fothergill (Cm 192)	Implemented	Law of Property (Miscellaneous Provisions) Act 1989 (c34)
165	Private International Law: Choice of Law Rules in Marriage (SLC 105) (HC 3)	Implemented	Foreign Marriage (Amendment) Act 1988 (c44)
164	Formalities for Contracts for Sale of Land (HC 2)	Implemented	Law of Property (Miscellaneous Provisions) Act 1989 (c34)
163	Deeds and Escrows (HC 1)	Implemented	Law of Property (Miscellaneous Provisions) Act 1989 (c34)
161	Leasehold Conveyancing (HC 360)	Implemented	Landlord and Tenant Act 1988 (c26)
160	Sale and Supply of Goods (SLC 104) (Cm 137)	Implemented	Sale and Supply of Goods Act 1994 (c35)
	1986		
157	Family Law: Illegitimacy (Second Report) (Cmnd 9913)	Implemented	Family Law Reform Act 1987 (c42)
	1985		
152	Liability for Chancel Repairs (HC 39)	Rejected	
151	Rights of Access to Neighbouring Land (Cmnd 9692)	Implemented	Access to Neighbouring Land Act 1992 (c23)
149	Criminal Law: Report on Criminal Libel (Cmnd 9618)	Rejected	
148	Property Law: Second Report on Land Registration (HC 551)	Implemented	Land Registration Act 1988 (c3)
147	Criminal Law: Poison Pen Letters (HC 519)	Implemented	Malicious Communications Act 1988 (c27)
146	Private International Law: Polygamous Marriages (SLC 96) (Cmnd 9595)	Implemented	Private International Law (Miscellaneous Provisions) Act 1995 (c42)

LC No	Title	Status	Related measures
145	Criminal Law: Offences against Religion and Public Worship (HC 442)	Implemented	Criminal Justice and Immigration Act 2008 (c4)
143	Criminal Law: Codification of the Criminal Law: A Report to the Law Commission (HC 270)	Superseded	See LC 177
142	Forfeiture of Tenancies (HC 279)	Rejected	
141	Covenants Restricting Dispositions, Alterations and Change of User (HC 278)	Implemented in part	Landlord and Tenant Act 1988 (c26)
138	Family Law: Conflicts of Jurisdiction (SLC 91) (Cmnd 9419)	Implemented	Family Law Act 1986 (c55), Part I
	1984		
137	Private International Law: Recognition of Foreign Nullity Decrees (SLC 88) (Cmnd 9347)	Implemented	Family Law Act 1986 (c55), Part II
134	Law of Contract: Minors' Contracts (HC 494)	Implemented	Minors' Contracts Act 1987 (c13)
132	Family Law: Declarations in Family Matters (HC 263)	Implemented	Family Law Act 1986 (c55), Part III
127	Transfer of Land: The Law of Positive and Restrictive Covenants (HC 201)	Rejected	
	1983		
125	Property Law: Land Registration (HC 86)	Implemented	Land Registration Act 1986 (c26)
124	Private International Law: Foreign Money Liabilities (Cmnd 9064)	Implemented	Private International Law (Miscellaneous Provisions) Act 1995 (c42)
123	Criminal Law: Offences relating to Public Order (HC 85)	Implemented	Public Order Act 1986 (c64)
122	The Incapacitated Principal (Cmnd 8977)	Implemented	Enduring Powers of Attorney Act 1985 (c29)
121	Law of Contract: Pecuniary Restitution on Breach of Contract (HC 34)	Rejected	
	1982		
118	Family Law: Illegitimacy (HC 98)	Implemented	Family Law Reform Act 1987 (c42)
117	Family Law: Financial Relief after Foreign Divorce (HC 514)	Implemented	Matrimonial and Family Proceedings Act 1984 (c42)
116	Family Law: Time Restrictions on Presentation of Divorce and Nullity Petitions (HC 513)	Implemented	Matrimonial and Family Proceedings Act 1984 (c42)
114	Classification of Limitation in Private International Law (Cmnd 8570)	Implemented	Foreign Limitation Periods Act 1984 (c16)
114	Property Law: The Implications of Williams and Glyns Bank Ltd v Boland (Cmnd 8636)	Superseded	See City of London Building Society v Flegg [1988] AC 54
	1981		
112	Family Law: The Financial Consequences of Divorce (HC 68)	Implemented	Matrimonial and Family Proceedings Act 1984 (c42)
111	Property Law: Rights of Reverter (Cmnd 8410)	Implemented	Reverter of Sites Act 1987 (c15)
110	Breach of Confidence (Cmnd 8388)	Rejected	
	1980		
104	Insurance Law: Non-Disclosure and Breach of Warranty (Cmnd 8064)	Rejected	

LC No	Title	Status	Related measures
102	Criminal Law: Attempt and Impossibility in Relation to Attempt, Conspiracy and Incitement (HC 646)	Implemented	Criminal Attempts Act 1981 (c47)
99	Family Law: Orders for Sale of Property under the Matrimonial Causes Act 1973 (HC 369)	Implemented	Matrimonial Homes and Property Act 1981 (c24)
	1978		
96	Criminal Law: Offences Relating to Interference with the Course of Justice (HC 213)	Rejected	
95	Law of Contract: Implied Terms in Contracts for the Sale and Supply of Goods (HC 142)	Implemented	Supply of Goods and Services Act 1982 (c29)
91	Criminal Law: Report on the Territorial and Extra-Territorial Extent of the Criminal Law (HC 75)	Implemented in part	Territorial Sea Act 1987 (c49)
89	Criminal Law: Report on the Mental Element in Crime (HC 499)	Rejected	
88	Law of Contract: Report on Interest (Cmnd 7229)	Implemented in part	Administration of Justice Act 1982 (c53); Rules of the Supreme Court (Amendment No 2) 1980
86	Family Law: Third Report on Family Property: The Matrimonial Home (Co-ownership and Occupation Rights) and Household Goods (HC 450)	Implemented	Housing Act 1980 (c51); Matrimonial Homes and Property Act 1981 (c24)
	1977		
83	Criminal Law: Report on Defences of General Application (HC 566)	Rejected	
82	Liability for Defective Products: Report by the two Commissions (SLC 45) (Cmnd 6831)	Implemented	Consumer Protection Act 1987 (c43)
79	Law of Contract: Report on Contribution (HC 181)	Implemented	Civil Liability (Contribution) Act 1978 (c47)
	1976		
77	Family Law: Report on Matrimonial Proceedings in Magistrates' Courts (HC 637)	Implemented	Domestic Proceedings and Magistrates' Courts Act 1978 (c22)
76	Criminal Law: Report on Conspiracy and Criminal Law Reform (HC 176)	Implemented in part	Criminal Law Act 1977 (c45)
75	Report on Liability for Damage or Injury to Trespassers and Related Questions of Occupiers' Liability (Cmnd 6428)	Implemented	Occupiers' Liability Act 1984 (c3)
74	Charging Orders (Cmnd 6412)	Implemented	Charging Orders Act 1979 (c53)
73	Report on Remedies in Administrative Law (Cmnd 6407)	Implemented	Rules of Supreme Court (Amendment No 3) 1977; Supreme Court Act 1981 (c54)
	1975		
69	Exemption Clauses: Second Report by the two Law Commissions (SLC 39) (HC 605)	Implemented	Unfair Contract Terms Act 1977 (c50)
68	Transfer of Land: Report on Rentcharges (HC 602)	Implemented	Rentcharges Act 1977 (c30)
67	Codification of the Law of Landlord and Tenant: Report on Obligations of Landlords and Tenants (HC 377)	Rejected	
	1974		
62	Transfer of Land: Report on Local Land Charges (HC 71)	Implemented	Local Land Charges Act 1975 (c76)

LC No	Title	Status	Related measures
61	Family Law: Second Report on Family Property: Family Provision on Death (HC 324)	Implemented	Inheritance (Provision for Family and Dependants) Act 1975 (c63)
60	Report on Injuries to Unborn Children (Cmnd 5709)	Implemented	Congenital Disabilities (Civil Liability) Act 1976 (c28)
	1973		
56	Report on Personal Injury Litigation: Assessment of Administration of Damages (HC 373)	Implemented	Administration of Justice Act 1982 (c53)
55	Criminal Law: Report on Forgery and Counterfeit Currency (HC 320)	Implemented	Forgery and Counterfeiting Act 1981 (c45)
53	Family Law: Report on Solemnisation of Marriage in England and Wales (HC 250)	Rejected	
	1972		
48	Family Law: Report on Jurisdiction in Matrimonial Proceedings (HC 464)	Implemented	Domicile and Proceedings Act 1973 (c45)
	1971		
43	Taxation of Income and Gains Derived from Land: Report by the two Commissions (SLC 21) (Cmnd 4654)	Implemented in part	Finance Act 1972 (c41), s 82
42	Family Law: Report on Polygamous Marriages (HC 227)	Implemented	Matrimonial Proceedings (Polygamous Marriages) Act 1972 (c38); now Matrimonial Causes Act 1973 (c18)
	1970		
40	Civil Liability of Vendors and Lessors for Defective Premises (HC 184)	Implemented	Defective Premises Act 1972 (c35)
35	Limitation Act 1963 (Cmnd 4532)	Implemented	Law Reform (Miscellaneous Provisions) Act 1971 (c43)
34	Hague Convention on Recognition of Divorces and Legal Separations: Report by the two Commissions (SLC 16) (Cmnd 4542)	Implemented	Recognition of Divorces and Legal Separations Act 1971 (c53); now Family Law Act 1986 (c55), Part II
33	Family Law: Report on Nullity of Marriage (HC 164)	Implemented	Nullity of Marriage Act 1971 (c44), now Matrimonial Causes Act 1973 (c18)
31	Administration Bonds, Personal Representatives' Rights of Retainer and Preference and Related Matters (Cmnd 4497)	Implemented	Administration of Estates Act 1971 (c25)
30	Powers of Attorney (Cmnd 4473)	Implemented	Powers of Attorney Act 1971 (c27)
29	Criminal Law: Report on Offences of Damage to Property (HC 91)	Implemented	Criminal Damage Act 1971 (c48)
	1969		
26	Breach of Promise of Marriage (HC 453)	Implemented	Law Reform (Miscellaneous Provisions) Act 1970 (c33)
25	Family Law: Report on Financial Provision in Matrimonial Proceedings (HC 448)	Implemented	Matrimonial Proceedings and Property Act 1970 (c45); now largely Matrimonial Causes Act 1973 (c18)
24	Exemption Clauses in Contracts: First Report: Amendments to the Sale of Goods Act 1893: Report by the Two Commissions (SLC 12) (HC 403)	Implemented	Supply of Goods (Implied Terms) Act 1973 (c13)

LC No	Title	Status	Related measures
23	Proposal for the Abolition of the Matrimonial Remedy of Restitution of Conjugal Rights (HC 369)	Implemented	Matrimonial Proceedings and Property Act 1970 (c45)
21	Interpretation of Statutes (HC 256)	Rejected	
20	Administrative Law (Cmnd 4059)	Implemented	See LC 73
19	Proceedings against Estates (Cmnd 4010)	Implemented	Proceedings against Estates Act 1970 (c17)
18	Transfer of Land: Report on Land Charges affecting Unregistered Land (HC 125)	Implemented	Law of Property Act 1969 (c59)
17	Landlord and Tenant: Report on the Landlord and Tenant Act 1954, Part II (HC 38)	Implemented	Law of Property Act 1969 (c59)
	1968		
16	Blood Tests and the Proof of Paternity in Civil Proceedings (HC 2)	Implemented	Family Law Reform Act 1969 (c46)
	1967		
13	Civil Liability for Animals	Implemented	Animals Act 1971 (c22)
11	Transfer of Land: Report on Restrictive Covenants	Implemented in part	Law of Property Act 1969 (c59)
10	Imputed Criminal Intent (Director of Public Prosecutions v Smith)	Implemented	Criminal Justice Act 1967 (c80), s 8
9	Transfer of Land: Interim Report on Root of Title to Freehold Land	Implemented	Law of Property Act 1969 (c59)
	1966		
8	Report on the Powers of Appeal Courts to Sit in Private and the Restrictions upon Publicity in Domestic Proceedings (Cmnd 3149)	Implemented	Domestic and Appellate Proceedings (Restriction of Publicity) Act 1968 (c63)
7	Proposals for Reform of the Law Relating to Maintenance and Champerty	Implemented	Criminal Law Act 1967 (c80)
6	Reform of the Grounds of Divorce: The Field of Choice (Cmnd 3123)	Implemented	Divorce Reform Act 1969 (c55); now Matrimonial Causes Act 1973 (c18)
3	Proposals to Abolish Certain Ancient Criminal Offences	Implemented	Criminal Law Act 1967 (c58)

Appendix B
The cost of the Commission

The cost of the Commission is met substantially from core funding provided by Parliament (Section 5 of the Law Commissions Act 1965) and received via the Ministry of Justice. The Commission also receives funding contributions from Departments towards the cost of some law reform projects, in accordance with the Protocol between the Government and the Law Commission.

	2015–2016 (April–March)		2016–2017 (April–March)	
	£000	**£000**	**£000**	**£000**
Commissioner salaries (including ERNIC)[1]	507.9		557.5	
Staff costs[2]	3210.3		3103.4	
		3718.2		3660.9
Research and consultancy	17.0		20.6	
Communications (printing and publishing, translation, media subscriptions, publicity and advertising) Design, print and reprographics Events and conferences (non-training) Information technology Equipment maintenance Library services (books, articles and online subscriptions) Postage and distribution Telecommunications	150.5		152.8	
Accommodation recharge (e.g. rent, rates, security, cleaning) (met by MoJ)[3]	663.5		643.1	
Travel and subsistence (includes non-staff)	37.0		26.0	
Stationery and office supplies Recruitment Training and professional bodies membership Recognition and reward scheme awards Childcare vouchers Health and Safety equipment/services	32.6		38.3	
Hospitality	0.2		0.0	
		900.8		**880.8**
TOTAL		**4619.0**		**4541.7**[4]

1 Excludes the Chair who is paid by HM Courts and Tribunals Service (HMCTS).

2 Includes ERNIC, ASLC, bonuses (not covered under recognition and reward scheme), secondees and agency staff.

3 In November 2013 the Law Commission moved to fully managed offices within the MoJ estate. This cost is met by MoJ directly.

4 Figures will form part of the wider MoJ set of accounts which will be audited.

Appendix C
Our business plan priorities for 2016-17

Priorities for 2016-17
Law Reform – to make a difference through law reform
We will: • Deliver law reform work that is high quality, to time and supported by a robust assessment of its impact, working in collaboration with stakeholders and in accordance with our Protocol, and we will support implementation of our law reform proposals. • Strengthen the knowledge and understanding of our special procedure internally, with officials in Whitehall, and in the Houses of Parliament, to support implementation of our law reform proposals. • Improve how we deliver the content of our publications to our stakeholders with a focus on accessibility, effectiveness and efficiency. • Begin the development of our 13th Programme of Law Reform, and continue to seek to attract additional references, to ensure the Commission has a balanced portfolio of work for this and future years.
Our People – to attract the best and continue to ensure the Law Commission is an excellent place to work
We will: • Have an organisational model which promotes more effective ways of working and which gives us more scope to be flexible with our resources. • Promote employee engagement in the corporate development of the Commission through effective internal communications. • Promote the health, safety and wellbeing of our staff, including through the organisation of events across the office and other initiatives. • Invest in our staff, developing their skills and knowledge, so that our capabilities remain aligned with our evolving business needs. • Put in place a strategy for maintaining our corporate memory and ensuring effective knowledge and information management.
External Relations and Reputation – to engage proactively with our stakeholders and respond to their feedback
We will: • Refine the framework for how – and why – the Law Commission presents itself to audiences. • Continue to use a range of media and activities to generate interest in and engagement with the work of the Law Commission, our consultations and our reports. • Maximise the potential of our online presence to enable engagement with our stakeholders, facilitate and encourage participation in our consultations and provide easy access to our reports and other papers.
Finance and Governance – to ensure decision making that is robust
We will: • Provide the administration necessary to support effective and efficient corporate performance which enables the Commission to deliver its objectives. • Agree and begin the implementation of our Spending Review settlement, deliver within the budget that we are set, and look to drive such further efficiencies as are possible. • Ensure the Commission, and its governing board, maintain high standards of corporate governance and continue to enhance our governance frameworks – including though the recruitment of a second non-executive board member.

Appendix D

Targets for 2016-17 and 2017-18

Targets for 2016-17

Target	Outcome
To publish reports on:	
Bills of Sale	Published on13 September 2016 (LC369)
Consumer Prepayments on Retailer Insolvency	Published on 14 July 2016 (LC368)
Event fees in Retirement Properties	Published on 31 March 2017 (LC373)
Enforcement of Family Financial Orders	Published on 15 December 2016 (LC370)
Form and Accessibility of the Law Applicable in Wales	Published on 29 June 2016 (LC366)
Insurance Contract Law: Insurable Interest	Project paused
Mental Capacity and Deprivation of Liberty	Published on 13 March 2017 (LC372)
Protection of Official Data	Carried over to 2017-18
Technical Issues in Charity Law	Carried over to 2017-18. Published on 14 September 2017 (LC375)
To publish consultations on:	
Misconduct in Public Office	Published on 5 September 2016 (LCCP 229)
Planning Law in Wales	Carried over to 2017-18. Published 30 November 2017
Sentencing Code	Carried over to 2017-18. Published on 27 July 2017 (LCCP 232).
Wills	Carried over to 2017-18. Published on 13 July 2017 (LCCP 231)

Targets for 2017-18

Target	
To publish reports on:	**To publish consultations on:**
Land Registration (Summer 2018)	Planning Law in Wales (November 2017)
Misconduct in Public Office (2018)	Search Warrants (Early 2018)
Protection of Official Data (September 2018)	Sentencing Code (Published July 2017)
Search Warrants (Late 2018)	Wills (Published July 2017)
Social Investment and Pensions (Published June 2017)	
Technical Issues in Charity Law (Published September 2017)	

Index of projects, Bills and Acts